Dare To

How to Climb Your Own Everest

By
Susan Harper

Rita, I know you'll get to the top of your Everest — & back down the other side ...♡ Girl Power is Real!

Susan Harper xxx.

For my parents and my brother for their unfailing love and support throughout my many adventures. Including the ones they didn't know about until afterwards!

And for Fred, with whom I shared many of my most memorable adventures and who gave me the courage and confidence not only to dare to dream, but to live those dreams.
He left us too soon…

About the Author

When Sue Harper stood on the summit of Everest in 2004 she was the first British woman to climb it as leader of an Everest Expedition. Only a handful of other British women had stood there before her. Sue has always been an adventurer and has also sailed the Atlantic Ocean and skied across the Alps from Austria to the Mediterranean.

Starting out life as a teacher, Sue put that career to one side when she stepped outside life's boundaries, challenging the limitations that are set for us by others and that we set for ourselves. Climbing Everest showed her that we are capable of much more than we think we are, and that the greatest risk of all is not daring to dream. Sue now works as an Intuitive Life Coach, passing on what she has learnt to others who have dared to dream and are climbing their own Everests in life.

INDEX

PREFACE

We all have our own Everests, our goals and dreams of what we want to do and how we want to live our lives. There is nothing to stop us achieving them, nothing except ourselves and our fear. We get frightened because taking on big challenges means showing our true colours, the part of ourselves that we have taken great care to hide away so carefully most of our lives.

Mountains, big challenges, are a true mirror of character. They make pretence or deception impossible and lay the soul bare. There can be no pretence when you are wobbling on the middle of a ladder across a bottomless crevasse, no hiding from who you really are. There is no middle way. It's either up or down.

I am often asked how I came to climb Everest; after all, not many women in the world have seen that incredible view from the highest point on the planet. My story is not an ordinary one, yet I am no more special than anyone else. This is a book for all those who, like me, know that there must be a greater purpose to their lives but don't know how to find it. It is for those who have a dream but don't know how to live it.

My own climb to the summit of Mount Everest is the heart and soul of this book. Woven into this story are the key principles by which I achieved my dream to show how everyone has within them the ability to climb their own Everest, to overcome challenges and to do things in life that they never dreamed possible. Because the greatest risk of all is not in aiming too high but in aiming too low.

HAVE YOU EVER HAD A DREAM?

Have you ever had a dream of doing something extraordinary, of becoming something else, someone else, really achieving something, giving meaning to your life, having a purpose instead of just 'being'? Wouldn't that be wonderful? Isn't that what we all dream of? But, more often than not, do you see these dreams as impossible, as things only other people do, not you? Only other people have successful businesses, only other people become millionaires, only other people can get out of the rut they've been in for years and turn their lives around, only other people sail across the Atlantic Ocean or climb Mount Everest...

But is the fact that you see these dreams as impossible simply an excuse for not trying? Isn't it easier to stay where you are, where it feels safe, in your rut, doing the job you don't like, in the unhappy marriage or relationship you can't seem to leave? Deep down inside, though, don't you have this nagging feeling that there is more out there for you, that you were born to do much more than you are doing right now?

Because, believe me, you were.

Your dreams are your possibilities. They come from the greater part of yourself. That's why we all have dreams, dreams of being something more than we are. They are our signposts, pointing the way to our future. You might think that your dream is impossible but, believe me, it is not!

Your dream might not necessarily be of doing something like climbing Mount Everest; it might simply be getting fit and climbing your local hill. But, if you've never had a pair of hiking boots on your feet before, just standing on the top of that hill would be like summiting Mount Everest. Or your dream could be changing your job, or simply getting a promotion. Maybe you work in an office but have always dreamed of becoming an artist or a writer or even a movie director.

Whatever it is, the question you have to ask yourself is why it is still a dream. Why hasn't it become reality? Why do we sometimes get to the brink of *nearly* taking that first step towards achieving our dream – maybe looking something up on the internet, looking at jobs or at college courses, imagining ourselves in that dream job, climbing that mountain, living with the man or woman of our dreams – then at the thought that it could become reality why do we quickly step back?

We step back from taking that first step because of fear, fear of the unknown and fear of change. It's easier to step back into what we know than to move forward into the unknown. When I was climbing Everest, and there was so little oxygen that I didn't feel as though I could breathe and my mind was telling me I was going to die with every step, it would have been much, *much* easier to turn around. It would have been *so* much easier to go back down than to go on, walking further into the Death Zone with every step, knowing that up there I could die. But I didn't turn round and I didn't die.

It is normal to be scared of change and of what is ahead of you, because you don't know what challenges you may face or whether you can cope with them. However when you get scared, more often than not you step back from the unknown into your comfortable habits, back to the nine-to-five job, the housework, the daily drudgery, back to the security of what you know even though you don't like it! You go back to living the dream in your head, back to reading about the exploits of others and how they achieved *their* dream, and back to living your dreams vicariously through them. You tell yourself that these are things that only other people do: special people, people with exceptional talents or from privileged backgrounds, people who are in some way very different from you. How on earth could you ever presume to imagine that *you*, with no special talents that you can see, could possibly live *your* dream?

And so life goes on being comfortably uncomfortable, until one day you feel an awakening of belief. You suddenly dare to think that maybe, just maybe, there could be a way. And so you give that dream a voice, and you tell someone about it – your partner, a friend, a colleague. And they look at you in astonishment and say, '*You*, climb the north face of the Eiger?' or '*You*, train as a lawyer?' or '*You*, become a psychiatrist? Don't you think maybe you need to *see* one, honey? Oh, and before you make the call, sweetie, could you get me that cup of coffee?'

Deflated, you crumple, curl up into a ball and that tiny bit of belief that dared to show its face evaporates before your eyes. The incredulity with which your idea was received confirms what you always thought, that dreams are just dreams. They are not the real world. The real world is where you get on with what you have always done, where dreams only become reality in *other* people's lives, where you have to make the best of your lot because it's all you'll ever have. It confirms the belief, the very limiting belief, that *you* can't turn your dream into reality and you can't change anything. That you can't change your life.

Well, I want you to turn that belief around and stand it on its head. I'm telling you right here and now that YES, YOU CAN. Yes, you *can* turn your dreams into reality. Yes, you *can* change your life. It's time to reclaim your power, your strength, your inner wisdom and your self-belief. Today, right now, you have permission to be *you*, the you who is going to turn your dreams into reality. And by *you* I mean who you really are.

Who is that, by the way? You may not actually remember because it's so long since you were last in touch with your real self. Think about it. When were you last really *you*?

When were you last really you? Do you even know who that is?

We spend much of our lives living in the image of others and being the person our partner, friends, even family, want us to be - so they will like us. In fact we spend so much of our lives being someone else, that as we grow up we lose sight of who we *actually are*. Which is the person, the child, that was born as a blank canvas, a beautiful, innocent baby, full of love, with not an iota of badness in its body. With no knowledge of words like bad, hatred, guilt, envy, jealousy... What happened to that person? That innocent child? Where did it go? Where did *you* go? Where did *I* go?

Yes, *me*. Because I also spent much of my life being someone else. I lost sight of who *I* really was. You see, we

5

become so good at being this other person, this alter ego, that we identify with them completely. We see this person as who we are, and for me it was all to do with fitting in with the crowd, wanting to be 'one of them' (whoever *they* were) not wanting to be different, or to stand out.

I actually felt it happening when I first went to high school. I didn't feel I fitted in with the other children. I came from a different background, spoke with a different regional accent, didn't like the same pop music they liked, and I was left out of their little cliques which hurt at that age. So, I changed myself. I modelled myself on them; I started to speak how they spoke. I said I liked the music they liked, and I pretended I liked and did all manner of things that I would never normally like or do just so I would fit in and they would like me.

Gradually I stopped being me and became someone else, my alter ego. Yes, I was still me underneath but I was putting on so many layers of falseness that gradually the real me began to be buried and I forgot who I'd ever been. Writing this now I feel sad at the things we will do to fit in, to be one of the crowd. We are so ashamed or afraid of our uniqueness, when in reality it is what we should be embracing because we *are* all different. We're meant to be different! It's people being different that makes the world the amazing place it is.

But when you are young, you generally want to fit in otherwise others make fun of you and tease you, even bully you, so you become someone you're not. And the more you identify with this false image of yourself, the deeper the hole you dig for yourself. The new you becomes someone other people meet, and that person becomes who they know and like. Suddenly it seems there is no way back. When you start having boyfriends or girlfriends, then you try hard to become the sort of person you think they will like. If you go on to marry them, you are stuck with this alter ego because that is who they have fallen in love with – and suddenly you're in one very big, deep hole although by this time you will have forgotten you were ever anyone else.

When your partner, friend, husband or wife crushes the dreams that you dared to voice, when they make negative comments about your hopes or aspirations, remember that they don't really know you. They only know the person you have allowed them to see. They don't realise that you have the strength to change, the strength to make powerful decisions. Even *you* may have forgotten, but for that niggling feeling inside that's trying to wake you up, to tell you that you have the power of choice, the power to change and the ability to take responsibility for your life. It is telling you that you have the power to be *you* – the person you were *born to be*.

As you gradually start to find this person again, to peel away the layers that you were hiding beneath, you will come to the startling but empowering realisation that you are capable of much, much more than you ever thought possible.

This is what happened to me. Don't forget that, even though I am the one writing this, I am no different from any of you. I am not special except in the way that we are all special. Just because I'm writing this doesn't mean that I'm perfect, or better than any of you in any way. In fact, if I were perfect and had lived the perfect life then I *wouldn't* be writing this because I wouldn't have anything to say! I wouldn't have learned the lessons from life that I now want to share with you. If I'd started out as perfection personified, I couldn't share with you how you can turn your life around and make it how you want it to be, how you can exchange the life you have now for something better if that's what you want. If I hadn't had to do it myself, I wouldn't know how. If I'd started out with everything I'd ever wanted, if I had been born with my dreams already realised, then I would have no idea how to go about achieving dreams and finding out that is possible. I would have no idea that dreams really can come true.

Dreams really do come true

It was because I not only dared to dream but dared to live that dream that early one Sunday morning I found myself standing on a very narrow ridge in the dark, almost 9,000 metres above sea level. All I could see in front of me were the few feet of rock and ice lit up by the beam of my torch but I could sense the huge drops on either side of me. It was a long way down.

Above my head stars were twinkling like diamonds in the black night sky. They had been keeping me company all the hours that I had been climbing. Now, at last, the sky was getting lighter and I knew the dawn was arriving. I was glad, for my toes were cold and I longed for the sun to warm them.

I looked to the east over Tibet, that beautiful country that I had visited the year before. As I watched, I saw the sun, a big red ball of light and hope, rising over the high Tibetan plateau. It was so indescribably beautiful that I was awestruck and emotional. This whole experience of climbing Mount Everest was so wonderful that I could hardly comprehend what was happening to me. Instead of feeling exhausted and frightened, like people told me I would, I was so excited that I wanted to jump for joy.

As it got lighter, I could see what lay ahead of me. By now I was on the South Summit and there in front of me was the steep rock corner of the famous Hillary Step. Beyond that was a wavy, very corniced snow ridge and I knew the summit was just along there. It makes me smile writing that, because 'just along there' makes it sound very easy, whereas it actually took about an hour and a half to reach. Up there, there is only thirty percent of the oxygen we have at sea level, so everything takes a long time because our muscles can't work quickly. Not only that, the lack of oxygen means that there is a high risk of dying.

On this mountain, my greatest challenge, I had to face that fear with almost every step. I had never been this high before. I was climbing into what is known as the Death Zone, so called because above 8000 metres there is so little oxygen that if something goes wrong, you are more likely to die than survive. I was taking a risk, the biggest risk I had ever taken.

I didn't know what would happen to me up there, whether my body could cope with the lack of oxygen, with climbing for fourteen hours without a break at over 8,000 metres, and with nothing to eat or drink because everything had frozen. I didn't know whether I would get frostbite and lose fingers or toes. I didn't know if I would survive. But I was willing to take the risk and I faced up to all my fears because I knew that if I didn't at least try, I would have no idea what I could do.

I'm sure people doubted that I could climb Everest – I'm not very big and not as strong as a lot of men. But

9

what counts is what you have inside you: the determination and belief you have in yourself.

I have seen strong men fail on Mount Everest, not because they found it physically too difficult but because they couldn't cope with their fears. They didn't believe in themselves; they had too many doubts. They had listened to all the people who told them how difficult it was and that they might die so they crumpled at the last hurdle, stepped back from the challenge into their comfort zone and found an excuse to turn around and go home – only to regret it.

Of course I had doubts that I could climb Everest; it's the highest mountain in the world and very few women had climbed it at that time. But I had learned that to get anywhere in life you have to take risks, which means stepping out of your comfort zone. When I looked at the mountain from below, it was dauntingly big, enough to make anyone turn tail and go home. Instead of doing that, I decided I would take it one day at a time. I wouldn't spend nights lying awake worrying about what might happen on summit day, I would just think about the next day, about getting to Camp One and then to Camp Two. By doing this, I eventually found myself climbing those final slopes, along that wavy corniced ridge and onto the summit of Mount Everest. I was achieving my goal, my dream.

As I was standing on the highest point on Earth, looking at the world laid out before me, in awe at its unbelievable beauty, I came to the sudden realisation that at last I had found myself. In doing something so difficult and dangerous, you can't be anything but yourself. Your guard is down and the mask is off. In that moment of recognition, I knew that the elusive something that I had been searching and striving for all my life, that I had always assumed was the right man, the right job, the perfect life, was in fact *me*. Here at last, on the summit of the world, I had found what I had always been looking for: I had found myself, the person I was born to be.

I took the risk, I dared to dream and it changed my life. I called on the strength, courage and will-power that we all have inside ourselves and I was astonished at my own resources. You have those same resources too; they are there for all of us.

Everything you could ever want, everything you could ever dream of doing, is waiting for you to believe that you can have it or do it. You just have to dare to dream.

Everyone has their own Everest, dreams of what they want to do or how they want to live their lives. There is nothing to stop you achieving those dreams except yourself, and remember that you have limitless potential. You – and only you – have the power within yourself to change things. So why not take that risk, step over that line and dare to believe that you can change your life?

Once you make the decision, look forward to life never being the same again. Look forward to it being more wonderful, fruitful and prosperous than you could ever imagine. It is there for the taking. You only have one go at this, so what are you waiting for? Dare to dream and be sure to dream big.

The summit pyramid of Mount Everest

PART ONE

I DARED TO DREAM

CHAPTER ONE

An End and a Beginning

Life is a journey. Where you are on that journey right now is a direct result of the choices you have made at every moment of your life. The decision to turn right, left or go straight on when you reached a crossroads has led you to this moment right now. Whichever direction you took was the right one because every experience in your life, whether good or bad, is one that you learn from.

None of this had ever entered my head when I sat at home, waiting for whatever was meant to happen to me to actually happen because I was certain that something should! I was sure there was something more, something important that I was meant to do in my life, but I had no idea what it was. I was equally sure that, if it was meant to happen, it would come and find me without me having to do anything. I thought the phone would ring or someone would come knocking on the door with news of what I was supposed to do next. Perhaps I would be asked to appear on TV (why for goodness' sake?!) and I would instantly become famous or ... I had no idea what!

So I just waited and waited. In the meantime being a good wife but at the same time becoming more and more frustrated that there *was* no knock on the door, no phone call, no signposts to show me the way.

Little did I know that I was actually in training for what was in store for me. At the time I was living the most amazing life in one of the most beautiful places I could imagine in the French Alps. My husband was a mountain guide and I could go climbing and skiing pretty much every day if I wanted to. It was truly wonderful – but it didn't seem to be enough. I still felt there was something missing. I was still thinking, 'I *know* I am born to do more with my life than live here having a wonderful time!'

Seems crazy, right? But I'm sure you know what I mean. I know that I am not the only person to have felt like this; I suspect that at some point in our lives, everyone feels like this. In fact, that could be why you are reading this book right now.

So I dabbled in this and that, hoping that the thunderbolt would arrive to illuminate the right road for me. I took people trekking in the mountains, I translated books and I wrote articles. I drank red wine, sipped *café au lait*, ate croissants and *pains au chocolats*... And all the while I was waiting.

***

When the thunderbolt did arrive to jolt me out of my rut, of course it was not what I had expected. My husband was diagnosed with cancer and in a flash I woke up. It was as if all those years of waiting I had been in a deep sleep, unaware of what I already had, always wanting something else, something more – even though I didn't know what that was. Suddenly life as I had known it was over and there was no going back. In a single moment, life had gone from being sunny and happy, full of laughter, the clink of wine glasses and the smell of fresh coffee amid the majestic, snowy mountains to one of darkness. Life became hospital wards, operating theatres, long bedside vigils, and then finally aloneness and uncertainty. At the age of thirty-nine, it felt as though not only my husband's life was over but mine was too.

I fell into a deep spiral of despair. I felt lost and alone, unable to see a way out of the dark tunnel in which I found myself. My confidence and sense of security vanished, seemingly overnight. Not only had I lost my husband but the job I had created for myself had disappeared overnight too: I was no longer a wife, I was a widow. I was out of a job and with it had gone the job security, which was my husband and the life I had made for myself with him.

I realised that I had been so busy being a wife that I had lost all sense of my own identity. Now I not only had no idea what to do but I had no idea who I was! I had always had boyfriends, and then a husband. I had never really been on my own and I was scared. I wasn't used to thinking for myself, having to make decisions that would affect my life. Big decisions, such as where did I want to live? What was I going to do? *Who was I going to be?*

Yes, my whole life was out there waiting for me. It was a blank canvas on which I could paint anything. That sounds wonderful – but I was absolutely terrified!

***

A year and a half later I knew I needed to do something positive to pull myself out of the black hole I was still in. I was stuck and needed to make a move; any move was better than doing nothing. Waiting led nowhere; I had learned that lesson well.

So, when an opportunity for an adventure presented itself, I knew I had to take it. Even though I still lacked confidence and felt insecure and scared, it was now or never. Deep inside I knew it was time to take charge of my life and start learning about who I really was.

The moment I made this decision and said yes to adventure, a realisation dawned: I suddenly saw that during all those years when I had been waiting for something to happen, waiting for the world to change, the world had been waiting for me.

CHAPTER TWO

The Adventure Begins

I had my nose glued to the window; any minute now, I was going to see my mountain. The air stewardess had told me that I would have the best view from the right-hand side of the plane. I was excited, even though it wasn't the first time I had seen Everest. There was something so special about it; just the thought of seeing it again made me feel emotional.

My thoughts drifted back to this time last year, when I had my first glimpse of the mountain known in Tibet as Chomolungma, which translates as Mother Goddess of the Earth. It had been on the flight from Kathmandu in Nepal to Lhasa in Tibet. That trip was a first for me in many ways, mainly because it was *my* trip. I was doing something because I wanted to do it, not because my boyfriend or my husband wanted to do it and I was just tagging along as the wife or the girlfriend adjunct. In fact, it was the first time for a very very long time that I had actually done something for myself, a big adventure that I really wanted to do. Wow! It was a frightening thought. For most of my life, I had been doing things either because other people wanted me to, or because I thought I should. No more, I decided. Enough.

I dragged myself back to the present … the past was gone and there was no point in dwelling on it. I focused my gaze on the view – how could I not? It was a clear day and there out of the window were the high Himalaya. The huge mountains seemed to be floating like islands in the sky with their summits above the clouds, while the rest of their huge mass lay out of sight below. It was breath taking and I was spellbound.

When the person in the seat behind me said, 'Look, there's Everest!' there was no need to ask 'Where?'. I had been worried that I wouldn't recognise it amongst the other Himalayan giants and that we would have passed it before I realised, but the sight of it made my gasp.

It was so big, quite literally head and shoulders above the rest. It was awe-inspiring and it took my breath away. It dwarfed every other mountain within sight, including its nearest neighbour Lhotse, which I knew was the fourth highest mountain in the world.

I looked, and for the umpteenth time in my life, fell in love. But this time it was different: it wasn't with a man, it wasn't a love based on any sort of conditions or bound up with guilt, or envy or jealousy. The love of a mountain isn't like that; it is an unconditional and permanent sort of love, one that takes up a place in your heart and never leaves.

I had always thought that there was nothing special about Mount Everest except the fact it was the highest mountain on the planet until I'd first seen it the previous year. I had seen pictures but I was unprepared for its effect on me when I saw it in its own environment. Nobody told me it was so beautiful. I was mesmerised, tantalised. It looked so high! I needed to touch this mountain, to feel it, to be it, to live it. To live with it.

Sitting on the plane looking out of the window at Everest, I wondered if it really was just a series of coincidences that I had decided I was finally ready for adventure and had gone back to the Alps, where I was immediately offered a job with a company that just happened to run expeditions to Everest.

But I had begun to realise that there was no such thing as coincidence. I was beginning to see that when I made a decision to do something and actually followed through on it, rather than just sitting waiting for the world to come to me, miraculous things somehow happened. I could only describe it as the universe conspiring with people and events to put the right pieces of the jigsaw together.

What had started out as just a thought, an idea, had actually become reality.

***

One year earlier, eighteen months after my husband died, I decided to step out of my comfort zone and say yes to adventure. I decided to go back to the Alps where I used to live to see some of my old friends and to do *something*, rather than sit at home doing nothing.

That decision was to change my life. The day I arrived back in the Alps, I climbed out of the black hole I seemed to have been in for so long and saw a glimmer of light at the end of the tunnel.

The first day I was there, I met an old friend who ran a mountain guiding company organising days out for climbers and skiers. He offered me a lifeline, a job in his office. For the first time for a long time I had something to do, to focus on, and I was surrounded by friends.

The company also ran Himalayan expeditions to Everest and other big mountains. One of the people working alongside me, Lou, was going with the company's expedition to climb Everest from the north side in Tibet. The border between Nepal and Tibet runs along the summit ridge of Everest and it can be climbed from both countries.

'Why don't you come on the trip too, Sue?'

I stared at Lou. Taking my look to be one of horror, he clarified. 'I don't mean to climb to the top but, as well as the main expedition going for the summit, we're also running a side trip which will just go as far as Camp One on the North Col. Why don't you come? It means you get to climb part of the way up Everest to 7000 metres.'

'Everest?' I thought. 'Tibet?' Far from horror, my response was amazement that I was being given a chance not only to see Everest but to climb part of the way up it.

Coincidentally, only a few weeks earlier I had met a friend, Polly, who had climbed Everest the year before, becoming the first Scotswoman and only the fourth British woman to summit the highest mountain on the planet. Talking to her about her amazing achievement, I had felt a twinge of envy as she told me how exciting and incredible her adventure had been. I could see it as she described it to me and I had felt a pull, a longing, a desire to experience it for myself. To go on an expedition, to visit the Himalaya and at least to see Everest, even if I couldn't climb it because climbing big mountains like Everest was something only other people did, definitely not ordinary people like me…

Yet here I was, only two weeks later, being offered the chance to go and see the mountain for myself. In fact not only to see it but to climb part of the way up it!

***

One year earlier, in the spring, I had flown to Tibet. It was all I had dreamt it would be. I had loved Lhasa, been speechless when I saw the Potala Palace so big, so beautiful, and so imposing. Tibet is a high plateau, arid for the most part, other parts covered in green pampas, with the huge Himalayan mountains rising up as a backdrop. It was quite literally breathtakingly beautiful.

The people were so lovely, dignified and welcoming. Many of them still lived as nomads on the Tibetan plains, in their tents with a few sheep. I was surprised how at home I felt there. It didn't seem strange to me; I almost felt as though I had come home, but I didn't understand why.

I loved all of it; the country had a special quality. Perhaps it was the rarefied atmosphere – after all, most of Tibet is above 3000 metres – the clarity of the air, the vast open spaces. There were so few people in that huge landscape.

One thing that had struck me in particular was the problem with language. It was the first time in my life, that I had been to a country in which I could not communicate at all. Having lived in France for twelve years, I speak several European languages but in Tibet they speak Chinese. I couldn't speak one word of Chinese and I hadn't a clue what any of the signs said, as the written language uses totally alien pictograms. I had never experienced this before.

One day I was out on my own in Lhasa and decided to get a taxi back to the hotel instead of walking, as it was quite a long way. I hailed a taxi and got in. 'Can you take me to the Snow Land Hotel, please?' I asked.

The taxi driver looked at my blankly.

'The Snow Land Hotel?' I repeated.

The taxi driver looked nonplussed and said something in Chinese. I realised he didn't understand a word I was saying and unfortunately I didn't have a clue what the name of the hotel was in Chinese. Unless I could find out, I was obviously not going to be going anywhere!

I had just decided I had better get out and walk, when the taxi driver set off, in what I was sure was the totally wrong direction. He took me to a hotel – but it wasn't mine. I shook my head and we looked at each other. Now I was completely lost. I couldn't even walk from here, because I no longer knew where I was.

I was beginning to get worried when the driver said something else and set off once more.

'Where on earth are we going now?' I thought anxiously. I didn't feel that I was going to come to any harm as I trusted these people, but I couldn't imagine how I was going to get back to my hotel. The taxi slowed down and drew up beside an old, fairly imposing building. To my surprise, the taxi driver got out of the car and went into the building. I looked at the sign on the railings; it read, in English, *University of Lhasa*.

What on earth were we doing here? I was about to find out. Ten minutes later, the driver appeared accompanied by a European-looking girl who turned out to be English, and was studying at the university. She asked me what the problem was and immediately translated the name of my hotel for the taxi driver.

I was profuse in my thanks both to the girl and particularly to the taxi driver. What ingenuity! To have thought of taking me there and then going to all that trouble of finding an English student to help me – I was very touched. It was just one example of what beautiful people the Tibetans are.

***

We reached Everest Base Camp and a few weeks later I found myself at 7000 metres on the North Col of Everest. I was loving every moment of this trip. The mountain was every bit as beautiful as I had imagined it to be, and more.

23

I cast a longing look back at the upper slopes of the mountain above me as I descended back to Base Camp, wondering what it was like up there, where the rest of the expedition was heading.

From Advanced Base Camp, the top of Everest is just visible. Very early the next morning, I looked through a telescope and saw my friend standing on the summit. Witnessing that moment had a profound effect on me. 'What must he be feeling, what must he be seeing, standing up there on the highest point on the planet?' I wondered.

When he got back to Base Camp, there was something imperceptibly different about him, something I couldn't quite put my finger on. I realised that an experience like that is life changing in ways you cannot articulate in words. It is something you feel with your heart and your soul, and I knew that whatever that feeling was I wanted to experience it. I didn't just want to come and look at the mountain, I wanted to climb to the top of it, see that wonderful view and experience the incredible feeling of achievement that must come from climbing the highest mountain in the world.

So I set myself the ultimate challenge and, for what felt like the first time in my life, I dared to dream.

***

Like all dreams, it was easier said than done. I'm sure you know what I mean. I had no clue where to start, all I had was a feeling, an overwhelming desire. I *so* wanted to climb that mountain and my heart was speaking to me, but I had no idea how I was going to get from where I was now to where I wanted to be. What I did know was that following my heart and my intuition had got me this far, so I was willing to take the risk and do it again.

On the plane back from Lhasa to Kathmandu, I threw my rule book of life out of the window. The rule book that said only extraordinary people do things like climbing Mount Everest, and I wasn't one of them. In that moment I stepped outside the boundaries and limitations that I had set for myself and started challenging the beliefs that went with them.

I had absolutely no idea how I was going to climb Mount Everest. It wasn't just the uncertainty that I could do it physically or whether or I had the mental strength; my greatest stumbling block was money. To climb Everest at that time cost a minimum of US$30,000–$40,000. Just to get a permit to set foot on the mountain cost $10,000. I didn't have that kind of money.

The new, unlimited me approached this problem in an unexpectedly different way. Before I threw my rule book out of the plane window I suspect I would have gone home and tried to work out in a very logical, left-brained way how on earth I could raise all that money. I would probably have written a lot of letters to potential sponsors – and drawn a blank.

This time, the creative part of me jumped in and I asked myself a question from the heart: 'SO … if I *was* going to climb Mount Everest what would be the next thing I would do?'

My answer was, 'Everest is the highest mountain on the planet (8848 metres high) so I'd better go and climb something fairly high to see if my body can cope with the lack of oxygen at high altitude. If it can't, and I don't feel good up there, then there's no point in trying to find the money.'

I listened to my heart instead of my head and, in order to test myself both mentally and physically at altitude, I signed up to go and climb an 8000 metre mountain in Tibet called Cho Oyu later that year. That expedition was going to cost me all the money I had in the world and I really felt I was taking a huge risk in several senses of the word. My mind was telling me constantly that I was crazy; not only could I die, but I was going to spend all my money on climbing a mountain when I could use it to do so many other more worthwhile, less frivolous, less dangerous things like living on it for a year or starting a business.

About a week before I was due to leave, I was sitting in the office where I worked in floods of tears. A friend walked in and asked me what on earth was the matter. I told her that I was about to spend all my money on climbing a mountain and if I didn't go then I would have all that money to do other things.

She looked me in the eye, bypassed my head and spoke to my heart. 'You can always earn money but you don't always get opportunities to do things like this. Follow your heart.'

I knew she was right and I had to trust I was doing the right thing. So I did.

I went to Tibet and climbed to more than 8000 metres on the mountain. It was tough but my body felt fine, so I knew I could cope with high altitude. And whilst I was there, I met and fell in love with a climber who was leading another expedition. Two years later we got married. And it just so happened that his job was running expeditions to climb Mount Everest and my wedding present was getting the chance to climb Everest. On my honeymoon! You could not make it up...

So in the end, because I listened to my heart and not my head and followed my intuition, I didn't need to find the money to climb Everest. It happened in a way I could *never ever* have dreamed of. Our mind does not know everything but our intuition does. Our mind only knows what it has learned; if I had listened to my mind, I would have sat at home trying to work out ways of raising money. Because I listened to what my intuition, my gut feeling, was telling me to do *and then did something about it,* I not only met my husband but I was given the chance to live my dream.

All I had to do now was to climb Mount Everest...

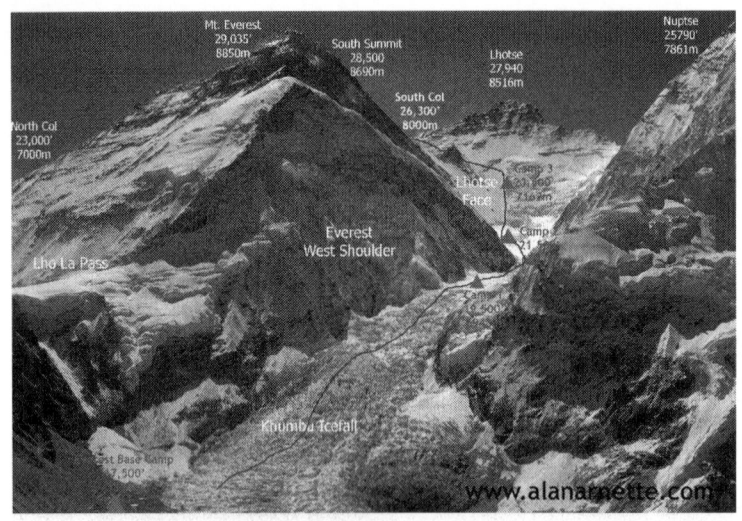

Courtesy of www.alanarnette.com © reproduction
prohibited without authorization

CHAPTER THREE

EVEREST DIARY

Base Camp
April 14th

Base Camp is in the most spectacular location. It is a sort of tented town set in a very large boulder field on a glacier. There is ice beneath the boulders, ice which is constantly moving because a glacier is quite literally a frozen river. In fact, I could hear it creaking and groaning last night as I lay in my tent trying to sleep.

The view that greets me every time I look out of the tent door is the famous Khumbu Icefall, which is not just a glaciated river but more a frozen waterfall, judging by the steepness of it. A jumbled mass of seracs (ice cliffs) and crevasses, it is the first obstacle every climber has to overcome on their way to the summit of Everest. And it is a major one, one that I know can be deadly, one that can cause climbers to question their commitment to this climb. If that commitment is not great enough, some go home. I haven't tested my own commitment by venturing into the icefall yet but I really want to have a closer look at it, to eyeball it, to talk to it, to question it and myself ... and then we'll see what the answer is.

For the most part the large crevasses in the icefall are too wide to jump across, so the larger gaps are bridged by ladders. Sometimes there is only one ladder but more often than not there are two, three, four or even more ladders tied together! This gives you an idea of how wide some of the crevasses are! The ladders are put in place by a group of sherpas known to expedition climbers as the 'Icefall Doctors'. Every expedition contributes some money towards this. We can't start climbing until the ladders have been put in place and the Icefall Doctors have found the safest route possible.

It is such a relief to at last be here at Base Camp, which will be home for goodness knows how many weeks – it could be six or seven. Exactly how long the expedition will last depends mostly on the weather and the time of our summit weather window. Over the last few years, the summit window has been in the latter part of May so it's likely I will be here until then, although I am hoping it will be really early this year...

By summit window, I mean the time when the weather is at its most clement, usually when the jet stream has moved away. It is the wind that is the most vital weather factor for good summit conditions. Everest is so high that its head is not only above the clouds but in the jet stream. The incredibly strong winds roar like an express train and apparently can be heard quite clearly from Camp Two, several thousand metres below the summit. I will soon be finding out for myself!

Base Camp and the Khumbu icefall

Face to face with the mountain
April 18th

We set off this morning for a first foray and face-to-face look at the icefall. It is about a twenty-minute walk from our camp to the start of the glacier. We weave in and out of boulders frozen into the ice and skirt round the tents of other expeditions. Even this short walk feels tiring to muscles unused to living at 5350 metres for any length of time. Hopefully they will be used to it soon!

When we stopped to put on our crampons at the bottom of the glacier I felt excited and nervous. After all the months of preparation and anticipation I was about to set foot in the famous Khumbu Icefall at last. Could I do this? Was I strong enough, good enough? Or was I kidding myself that a girl like me, an ordinary girl and an ordinary climber, could climb the highest mountain in the world? Well, we were about to find out.

It is about another twenty-minute walk across narrow crevasses and snow bridges to the first ladder. Just walking up the bottom part of the icefall was tiring. My muscles definitely weren't getting as much oxygen as they were used to and my speed seemed to be slow, or very slow; going fast at altitude was not possible right now!

The bottom part of the icefall is like a frozen sea and seems to resemble gentle, frozen waves, whilst higher up there are massive blocks of ice. It is definitely a frozen waterfall … a very high steep waterfall. Yikes! And we are going to climb through this jumble of ice up to Camp One in a few days' time. In fact, we are going to have to go up and down it about five times in total. Moving through it definitely concentrated the mind, particularly when I set my crampon-shod foot on the first wobbly ladder.

The crevasse we were practising on thankfully was not very wide and there were only two ladders tied together over a very deep drop of *only* about 100 feet – some crevasses are much deeper!

The ladders are anchored at each end with big metal ice stakes. There are loose ropes draped along each side of the ladder, which you clip into so that if you fall off, you will dangle rather than fall. The ropes are loose because the glacier is constantly moving downhill – it is, after all, a frozen river – and if the ropes were tight they would snap with the forward motion of the ice. However, loose ropes don't offer a lot of support, so it helps to have a buddy with you who can pull the ropes tight whilst you walk gingerly and slowly across the ladder. It is extremely tricky to place your feet on the rungs with crampons on your boots as the spikes get in the way, so the whole process feels very precarious and nerve-wracking. Goodness knows how many ladders we are going to have to cross going up to Camp One, but we are definitely going to get a lot of ladder-crossing practice!

This afternoon we have been packing for our first trip to Camp One. We are having breakfast at 3am and leaving in the dark at 4am so we can climb as much as the icefall as possible before the sun hits and starts to melt the ice. I'm nervous. I have a lot to carry – sleeping bag, sleeping mat, food, stove, pans, spare clothes, water – and I'm not sure how I will manage. I will know soon enough.

Sue crossing ladders in the icefall

Avalanche
April 21st

Yesterday I was shown just how dangerous this mountain really is. I nearly died in an avalanche.

Early in the morning at Camp One everything was silent when suddenly there was a huge roar from the shoulder of Everest. It got louder and louder, and nearer and nearer. I knew it was an avalanche.

I was sharing a tent with Vicky and we just grabbed each other. There was nothing else to do. I have rarely felt so helpless. Trapped in the tent, we couldn't run – which was what I wanted to do. I had no idea if I was about to die. Then suddenly the tent was flattened on top of us and I heard people screaming.

I was waiting for the weight of snow from the avalanche to start crushing us when the tent stood up again, only to be flattened again a few seconds later.

And then there was silence.

When it became obvious that we were going to survive, Vicky and I relaxed our grip on each other, swore a few times in relief and peered out of the tent. A short distance away I could see where the avalanche had dumped hundreds of tons of snow but thankfully not quite reached our tents.

We are now recovering back at Base Camp. We will be resting for a few days, going back up to Camp Two for a few nights, then descending to Base Camp for another rest. After that, we will go up to Camp Three for a night and back to Base Camp yet again. Then we wait nervously for a summit window….

The reason for all this yo-yoing up and down the mountain is because the body needs time to acclimatise

35

gradually to climb a mountain this high. As we make our way up the mountain, which is indescribably vast, we spend a few days at each new camp to give our bodies a chance to get used to the fact there is even less oxygen than there was at the camp below! Then we descend to the relatively thicker air of Base Camp to allow our bodies to recover. I say relatively thicker air because even at Base Camp there is still only 50% of the amount of oxygen that we breathe at sea level.

There are four camps in total. Camp Four is on the South Col, a col being a flat area of land between two mountains. In this case, the mountains are Everest and the fourth highest mountain in the world, Lhotse. We will make our summit attempt from Camp Four but, as it is at 8000 metres and consequently difficult to reach, we won't be going there until we make our summit bid.

However, I'm jumping ahead of myself here. Before we go back up the icefall again, there are a few things I need to sort out between me and myself.

Coming face to face with myself
April 22nd

This first ascent of the icefall was hard. I knew it could take any time between five and eight hours and that it was pretty normal to feel dreadful, which it did and I did!

It was freezing cold and dark leaving base camp so early but as soon as the sun hit the snow and ice it was like being in a furnace, with the heat of the sun being reflected off every available surface. In the space of a few minutes I went from wearing every available item of clothing and wondering if my toes were going to get frostbite, to stripping off to my thermal underwear, donning sunscreen and a sun hat and wondering if I was going to get sunstroke! It was an incredible contrast.

In that heat, Camp One never seemed to get any nearer. When I thought I must be near the top I kept asking people coming down how much further it was – and I got a different answer from everyone!

Finally I arrived. Last. When we left Base Camp and started climbing up the icefall, all the team had been together. I spent the first hour trying to keep up and go at the same pace as everyone else but I got so out of breath that I knew I couldn't keep moving that quickly. Everyone time I stopped for a rest someone overtook me. The problem was that my rucksack was really heavy and I wasn't used to carrying so much weight. I felt as though I was being thrown off-balance on every horizontal ladder and on the vertical ladders the weight was dragging me backwards.

I knew I had to do something about it. If I was finding it difficult carrying everything this low down the mountain, how was I going to manage several thousand metres higher up where there was even less oxygen? The answer was that I wasn't!

I had got myself into this situation by 'trying to be one of the boys', which to me meant proving I was as strong and as fast as the men on the expedition, by carrying what they were carrying and moving at the same speed. But I wasn't a boy, was I? I was a girl! It was time to admit to myself that I wasn't as strong as them, not physically anyway. I was pretty sure I could give them a run for their money mentally.

On that first trip up the icefall, I not only came face to face with the mountain but I came face to face with the person I had been hiding away for more years than I could remember whilst pretending to be someone I was not. That person was myself: my *real* self.

If I wanted to climb this mountain, I was going to have to come out of hiding and embrace the person I really am. And that possibly meant a few difficult conversations with the person closest to me, my husband who had actually never met that person, not to mention a few raised eyebrows from the others on the team. But I knew that it was the only way forward; it was time to get out of my own way.

Dealing with fear
May 10th

I stopped and tensed as the ladder I was standing on suddenly tilted sideways slightly, not enough to throw me off it but enough to terrify me. I realised that the anchors must be loose.

I pulled the rope towards me as hard as I could. There were four ladders tied together across this giant crevasse and I was at the start of the third one, right in the middle. I didn't dare look down beyond my boots but I could sense a lot of space beneath my feet.

I dragged my focus back up from the ladder rungs and quickly scanned the glacier to see if there were any other climbers nearby who could help me, but there was no one around. All I could hear was the occasional rock falling – and silence. We were on our last trip up the mountain, on our way to the summit. We were all going at our own speed and I knew we were spread out across the mountain between Base Camp and Camp Two.

I had got used to crossing ladders on my own, and I knew how to pull against the ropes on each side to create tension and a vague sense of security, but I would be very glad never to set foot on a ladder across a crevasse ever again. It was frightening and the danger was palpable.

I realised I was holding my breath, which didn't help at this altitude because little enough oxygen was getting into my body as it was. I took a deep breath and shifted my weight sideways slightly to try and stop the ladder tilting so much. I told myself I was on my own and I could do this; there was no way I was going to die now, when all our acclimatisation and a lot of the hard work was done, and I was finally on my way to the summit.

Or then again, maybe I was going to die…

Suddenly, out of the silence, there was a huge roar from the slopes of Nuptse, the mountain towering above me on my right. 'Great, I'm going to be swept into a crevasse by an avalanche!' I thought as I panicked. For the second time on this mountain, there was nothing I could do but pray as I looked up and saw a cloud of snow spilling down the side of Nuptse from its upper slopes.

I didn't stop to think about the tilting ladder any more. My feet moved, my body seemed to know how to balance and I was on the other side of the crevasse in seconds as snow poured down the mountain face onto the glacier, but thankfully a hundred or so metres in front of me.

My legs felt wobbly. I threw my rucksack on the ground and collapsed on top of it, taking deep gulping breaths as I tried to slow down my racing heart. Moving quickly at 6400 metres, even for a very short way, takes a lot of effort and running ten meters is like sprinting a hundred!

As I got my breath back and tried to recover my equilibrium, I surveyed my surroundings: the majestic, awe-inspiring Western Cwm. Despite the evident dangers, I felt so lucky to be in one of the most beautiful places in the world on one of the most beautiful mountains in the world. No amount of superlatives could possibly convey the beauty and the splendour of it all. Every time I came up here, it never failed to take my breathe away – what little breath I had left, that is.

I craned my neck and looked up. Today there was a plume of cloud coming off the top of Everest so it must be windy up there on the summit. It seemed so far away but, then again, it was! Approximately 3000 metres above me.

I sighed, thinking once again about the distance from the top camp at the South Col to the summit. Not for the first time, I was assailed by doubt. There was no getting away from the fact that it was a very long way, even by my standards. I knew I had stamina – but did I have enough?

The summit wasn't somewhere I had let myself think about much because it had scared me when I first saw how far away it was. It looked so daunting that I doubted I had it in me to achieve it. I had experienced big mountain days in the past in the Alps and on Cho Oyu in Tibet, but summit day would be longer and harder than anything I had ever done before. I didn't know if I would have the physical and mental strength to get through it.

However, I knew that constantly thinking about it would not help because I didn't know exactly what I would be faced with until I was actually there. All I could do was to prepare my body and my mind the best I could.

It's all very well saying you are going to climb Everest – it's easy to say the words – but it's a whole other ball game doing it. I knew full well that many people who make grandiose claims about climbing Everest return home with their tails between their legs having decided it's not for them. They have to make excuses to their friends and family that they were ill, that they injured their leg, that they couldn't acclimatise to the altitude, that they didn't get on with the other members of the team, that they were homesick…

But, I wondered, why is it that the one reason no one ever gives is fear? That the task they had set themselves one night in the bar with their friends, is much more enormous than they realised? They had got themselves fit, bought all the equipment, paid for the best sherpas; they had oxygen, they had guides, they had everything ... except the ability to conquer their fears. And, as I well knew, there was plenty to fear up here. I had already experienced it.

It isn't conquering fear that matters, it is confronting it. Once fear is confronted, it often evaporates because in reality there is nothing to fear.

Fear is a perception of the mind; once you actually face the thing you fear and it becomes real, more often than not you can cope with it. Fear makes you turn around instead of succeed, turn away from challenges in case you fail. Fear makes you become someone else instead of yourself because you are afraid others won't like who you really are. Fear can control your life.

I looked up again towards the summit and that plume of cloud streaming off it. I didn't want to be one of those people who turned around and went home but there was no way of knowing whether or not I would be. I had absolutely no idea what was ahead of me; all I knew was that the higher I climbed the further out of my comfort zone I moved. And it wasn't just my comfort zone I was stepping out of, it was any zone I had ever known! I was stepping into the unknown and heading to a place very few people had ever been.

On the way to Camp One (Credit Mike Davey)

Mental Strength

I would suggest that only those people that have great mental strength generally succeed. Those that have the will and mental strength to push themselves where not many others have gone before. Not many out of the millions of people on this Earth have stood on the summit of Mount Everest. None of us knows what climbing to 8,848 metres will do to our bodies and our minds. Can we push our bodies that far, that high? Will we get frostbite, succumb to lack of oxygen or physical exhaustion? Will we die? All these doubts have to be mentally overcome on the way to the summit. If we cannot deal with them, then our minds will find an excuse for turning back.

Of course some people do have genuine life-threatening physical difficulties and have to turn around, and there are others who decide the risks are not worth taking, that there are other things in their lives more important than climbing Everest, and no one can blame them. In order to climb Mount Everest you have to *really* want it.

It is not a mountain to be underestimated, yet I believe some people do so because it has become commercialised, because you can pay to climb it without having been a climber all your life, because a slightly-built girl like me can climb it – but that doesn't make it easy. That doesn't mean it won't be the hardest thing you will ever do in your life.

Camp Two
May 11th

Camp Two is a cold cheerless place perched a on rocky moraine on the left side of the Western Cwm directly below the summit of Everest. From here you can tell when the jet stream is blowing across the summit because you can hear it roaring like a train, a constant unceasing noise. It's frightening because it is so loud, even 2500 vertical metres below the summit. What on earth must it be like up there? That's why we can't even think of trying to summit if there is a chance it's going to be very windy.

Camp Two is nothing more than a jumble of rocks amongst the ice. None of the tents are pitched anywhere very flat so sleeping here is pretty uncomfortable. And it freezing cold! The only way I can keep warm at night is to use two sleeping bags, one inside the other, and even then I have to wear my hat. The whole experience is really quite miserable.

The views are spectacular but up here at about 6,400 metres it's always difficult to sleep. It is usual to get a headache, feel nauseous and lose your appetite when you first arrive at this altitude. After a few days these symptoms generally go away as your body makes more new red blood cells to transport what little oxygen there is more efficiently and you start to acclimatise.

However, no matter how acclimatised you are, moving around at this altitude is still exhausting. It takes all your strength just to get dressed and you get completely out of breath doing something like packing up a sleeping bag. And going to the loo... well... At Base Camp there is a toilet tent with fairly rudimentary facilities, but at least there is some privacy. The toilet there is a barrel sunk into the rock with a toilet seat on top of it. It does get a bit smelly and as little time is spent in there as possible! It is removed whenever it gets full (don't think about it), taken away by a porter (what a job) and replaced with a new one – which is a good time to use it. Only a few days ago, just before we left Base Camp, one of the other expedition members dropped his glasses into the toilet barrel; they were his reading glasses, so he had to fish them out and disinfect them...

At Camp One, there are no toilet facilities, just a very low snow wall. You take a shovel and dig a hole behind the wall which is not much fun, particularly for the girls. Here at Camp Two, the toilet is a crevasse; there is no tent around it, just a crevasse. At Camp Three, on the Lhotse face, the facilities are zero and it is so steep that you have to be clipped to a rope at all times whatever you are doing! Whoever said climbing mountains was fun?

I was missing home and longed for the simple pleasures of a bath, a comfortable bed and a good cup of coffee. I thought about my parents, who I knew were away on holiday. I hadn't told them that I was coming to climb Everest as I knew they would worry; I had just told them that I was trekking to Base Camp and would probably stay on for a while. All of which was true! I *had* trekked to base camp and was staying for a while. I was just doing a bit extra that's all – like going to the summit.

Lying in my bed at Camp Two, wrapped up in every item of clothing I had with me, I told myself that it wouldn't be long. I counted the days. Tomorrow was a rest day. The following day, Wednesday, I was going to Camp Three and on Thursday to Camp Four on the South Col. All being well, on Thursday evening I would set off for the summit. I would spend Friday night at the South Col again, and on Saturday I would come all the way back down here to Camp Two. On Sunday I would descend the icefall for the very last time back to Base Camp and safety.

I knew that, even if I got to the summit, I wouldn't have actually climbed the mountain until I was back at Base Camp because that is the only place on the whole mountain that is safe. It would then take about three days to walk from Base Camp to Lukla, where I could catch a small plane back to Kathmandu. Hopefully I could get on a plane home immediately. I counted on my fingers: in two weeks' time, I should be back home. What a wonderful thought! It immediately cheered me up.

I pulled the sleeping bags up over my head in an attempt to keep out the cold and tried to go to sleep.

Sue dressed for the summit

May 12th

Today was spent trying on equipment and the clothing I was going to wear on summit day. Everything had to be right; I couldn't risk forgetting anything crucial like a head torch or mittens, as that would mean the end of my summit attempt.

I also needed to know exactly what clothing I would wear because I could only carry what I needed to the South Col. It was going to be very hard climbing up there because of the altitude, so I had to make sure my rucksack was as light as possible. I'm not built for carrying heavy loads … an issue that has already been addressed!

I got out all my clothing. When I was fully dressed in my summit outfit, I looked like a spaceman! All the summit-bound team were doing the same and it caused a lot of laughter. I had three layers of clothing on my bottom half and four on my top half, and over all that I had a big all-in-one down suit which felt wonderfully warm. I should have been wearing it in bed, though if I did I probably wouldn't fit inside my two sleeping bags!

On my feet I had big double boots with special insulation and a heated insole with a lead which is attached to a battery pack. The lead goes up my boot and up my leg inside my down suit, and the battery pack goes in my pocket to keep warm. This would hopefully stop the batteries from freezing, as well as my feet.

The only thing that I was really worried about was getting frostbite. I knew I could do the technical climbing and I was pretty good at altitude, but above 8000 metres it is cold. Very cold. I was going to nearly 9000 metres, to 8848 to be exact, and at that altitude it could be minus thirty centigrade. I did not want to lose any toes or fingers.

I love walking in the hills and I also love to play the piano, so for me no mountain was worth the loss of fingers or toes. I had taken every precaution.

I had crampons strapped to my boots and a climbing harness on top of my down suit. Attached to my climbing harness was a metal clip called a karabiner and a jumar, a friction device that you can slide up a rope but not down it. When you pull down, the jumar jams thus allowing you to haul yourself up. It's very useful for climbing steep ice faces, which is what I was going to be doing the following day.

The climbing sherpas, who are employed by every expedition, fix ropes up the route to the summit to make it safer. Even so, people still die every year because they think they are expert enough not to have to clip into the rope, then something unexpected happens – perhaps they slip or a piece of ice hits them on the head and they fall. Once you start falling on this mountain, you don't stop. It's steep.

I didn't need telling twice; there was no way I wouldn't clip the rope. I really didn't want to die and besides, my parents didn't know I was there...

On my hands I would have big mittens with thin gloves underneath. The mittens were attached to my wrists with cord like children sometimes have to stop them losing their gloves. I would have to remove my mittens to clip and unclip my karabiner and jumar and I couldn't risk losing them. On my head was a hat and a head torch, and over my face was an oxygen mask. I would also have ski goggles on my hat ready to put on the minute the sun appeared. The sun is so bright at that altitude that snow blindness is a real risk unless your eyes are well protected.

I could hardly move wearing all that paraphernalia and I was going to have to climb to the summit in it! The worst thing was the oxygen mask. It covers the whole of the face, except the eyes, and has a valve that sticks out at the front so I couldn't see my feet unless I bent my head really far forward. That was going to make it very tricky climbing the rock steps that I knew were up there. But I would manage somehow.

I had used oxygen before when I climbed on Cho Oyu, the mountain that I went to in Tibet the autumn after I'd climbed to the North Col of Everest. On Cho Oyu, I had found using the oxygen mask difficult at first because it felt as though I were suffocating. I kept taking it off but eventually I realised that it really was helping me and I got over my fear of suffocation. However, I remembered the problems I'd had seeing my feet – and that was on fairly easy terrain. Wearing an oxygen mask here was going to be interesting, to say the least.

I took everything off and packed it carefully into my rucksack making sure I didn't forget anything.

I was apprehensive about the following day as I was going to Camp Three - for the first time. Camp Three on the Lhotse face is very exposed to avalanche and, for that reason, none of the sherpas will stay there. That didn't fill me with confidence. Our climbing team had been scheduled to spend a night at this camp earlier in the expedition but we had been beaten back by bad weather. High winds, snow and freezing temperatures meant we were unable to move from our tents at Camp Two for four or five days. When we eventually tried to get to Camp Three, we were beaten back at the bottom of the ice face by the wind and the cold. It was pretty desperate. So, not having been up there I had absolutely no idea what to expect.

I was also well aware that once I left Camp Two early the next morning, I really was on my way to the summit. I was definitely nervous; it suddenly felt as though I was coming to the moment that my whole life had been about.

It felt surreal that I should be here on Everest at all. How on earth had I got here? There are so many climbers who dream all their lives of climbing Everest, and somehow I, Susan Harper, had managed to get here. Somehow everything seemed to have fallen into place. Now there was only one piece of the puzzle missing – and I suspected it had my picture on it.

Sue climbing the Lhotse Face to Camp Three (Credit Robert Jen)

Camp Three
May 13th

We got up at four o clock – it's a long way to Camp Three. It must have been minus twenty degrees centigrade and it seemed to take ages to get dressed into my warm clothes. I wasn't wearing my down suit yet, that was for summit day. It would be too warm to wear down here. I got out of breath just trying to stuff my sleeping bag into its sack, and by the time it was done my fingers were freezing and I had to put my gloves on for five minutes to try and warm them up again.

I couldn't really eat much breakfast, just a small bowl of porridge by the light of my torch. It was too early for food, but I knew I would be hungry later so I made myself eat it. At Camp Two there is a kitchen tent with a cook and cook boy. The kitchen has to be kept regularly stocked with food and has big gas primus stoves and gas bottles, all of which have to be carried up the icefall by the Sherpas. Yet more work for them to do. Plus there is no running water, so snow and ice have to be melted and then boiled, and this of course requires a lot fuel. Melting snow and ice is very time consuming, but it is just something that has to be done.

I put some energy bars and a bit of chocolate into my pocket and poured some hot water into my bottle, making sure it was full. I stuffed that inside my jacket for the time being; I would leave it there until the sun came out because, if I had it in my rucksack, it would immediately freeze. I also had a radio with me so I could keep in touch with Base Camp. I had been given a weather forecast the previous evening, which was that there would be some wind today, but not too much.

54

The whole team left Camp Two at 6 a.m. The first part of the route was over a gently rising glacier which led to the foot of the Lhotse face. Although it didn't look very far, it actually took me two hours. I found it quite hard going with the altitude and, as usual, I seemed to be going more slowly than the others, but my body just could not go any faster. At this altitude the muscles ge a lot less oxygen and it's very noticeable. However, I felt much better once I was on the fixed ropes on the Lhotse face, probably because I could see I was making some progress. On the flat of the glacier nothing ever seems to get any nearer, whereas on the steep ice face progress was more evident even though the climbing was more strenuous.

Clouds started swirling around me and I hoped it wasn't going to snow. Climbing the Lhotse face was hard enough work without having a blizzard to contend with. At each rope anchor I had to clip my jumar to the rope and then clip in the safety karabiner, pull up on the jumar and haul myself up. The ice under foot was very hard and I had to make sure the spikes of my crampons were firmly in it so I didn't lose my footing. It required unrelenting concentration and focus.

As I got higher and the view got more and more incredible, I realised with a feeling of elation that the clouds that had been around me were all now below me. Instead of feeling exhausted, out of breath, fed up and cold, and wondering where Camp Three was, I started to feel excited. Now at last, after all these weeks of trudging up and down the icefall and the Western Cwm, I felt as though I was actually climbing this mountain. My spirits lifted with the rising altitude and I had this huge feeling of excitement. Tears blurred my vision and overflowed down my cheeks. The view was so stupendous, and the feeling of space was overwhelming. The only way I could express how I felt was to cry.

Each expedition has their tents at Camp Three in a different location spread over quite a wide area. It took me half an hour to climb from the lowest tents to where I knew I would find ours much higher up the face. It was a drag when I was tired and getting cold, but I knew that I would be glad in the morning because I would have quite a head start on those climbers in the tents lower down. I looked up and saw those in our team who were ahead of me stepping out of the track and clipping into ropes beside a group of tents which I knew must be ours. Thank goodness!

The night I spent at Camp Three was without a doubt the worst I have ever had. I was sharing a tent with Vicky, who had experienced the avalanche with me at Camp One. The ice platform that our tent was perched on was by no means flat; in fact, it seemed to be undulating like frozen waves on the sea. One end of the tent was completely buried in the snow, and when I tried to get in the other end I found it was blocked up with oxygen bottles. At least there was plenty of oxygen!

It took us a while to sort everything out, get into the tent and move oxygen bottles around so we had space to lay out our sleeping bags. I was really tired. It had been a long day. But it wasn't over yet. We had to collect some snow in a bag, find the stove and pan, light the stove and melt the snow so we could have a drink and some food.

It is vital to keep well hydrated at this altitude; if you don't, it's easy to succumb to altitude sickness, which can be deadly because it's very difficult to rescue anyone this high on the mountain. Collecting snow to melt wasn't a problem – all we had to do was to unzip the end of the tent which was buried in the snow and scoop some into a pan! Well, that bit was easy but it was hard finding somewhere flat to stand the stove either inside or outside the tent. No part of the tent floor was flat and the ground outside the tent sloped!

While I was trying to sort all this out, Base Camp came on the radio and told me that the sherpas would be with us at eight o'clock the following morning and that the weather forecast was still good. Lucky them being down in nice warm Base Camp, I thought. I would never normally have thought of Base Camp as warm but it would be compared to where I was.

I blew on my fingers to warm them, as I fumbled with the lighter to get the stove going. We eventually stood it on a pan lid to try and keep it upright and I just had to hope it didn't fall over.

With all the oxygen bottles crammed into the tent, it was impossible to stretch out properly. I was going to use one of the bottles tonight because sleeping with oxygen would help me have a much better sleep – if I could sleep with an oxygen mask on, that is.

I picked up one of the oxygen bottles, found my mask and regulator and screwed the regulator on to the top of the bottle. The regulator controls the flow of oxygen between the tank and the mask. The greater the flow, the less time the oxygen in the bottle lasts and vice versa. There was a loud hiss as it connected. I put the mask to my face and breathed deeply. That was better. No matter how awful it was having the mask on, oxygen was definitely coming out of it and it did make a difference. I felt myself reviving as I kept the mask to my face.

Before it got dark I opened the tent door and looked out. I felt as though I was perched on an eyrie like an eagle about to take off. I was now at 7,300 metres, so high above the Western Cwm that the tents of Camp Two were just tiny dots. I felt as though I was in my own tiny cocoon up there. The sun had set leaving a red glow on the horizon and the sky was a pale blue. There was not a breath of wind. It was very cold, and very beautiful.

I looked across to the neighbouring mountain of Nuptse. I was nearly as high as its summit ridge, which was at 7861 metres. It was so wonderful to be here.

After all those weeks of gazing up at Camp Three and wondering what it was like, I was here at last. What an amazing feeling!

The summit ridge above the Hillary Step (Credit Mike Davey)

Camp Four
The South Col
May 14th

I woke very early the next morning. Actually, I didn't need to wake up because I hadn't slept. It was the most uncomfortable night I'd ever had in my life. I had been freezing cold even with all my clothes and my hat on, and there seemed to be huge lumps underneath the tent floor so I couldn't get comfortable. Whenever I moved I hit my elbow, knee or some other part of my anatomy on those damn oxygen bottles.

I had breathed oxygen for most of the night and wearing the mask hadn't helped, either. I was just glad it was now morning. The sun wasn't up as it was only five o clock, but I knew it would get here much earlier than it did at Camp Two down in the frigid Western Cwm. I was perched up here with the gods and the sun would be shining on us soon, then I could spread my wings and fly from my eyrie on up the mountain.

Today was a big day. Today, I was going to the South Col. Just saying those words, 'the South Col', gave me such a feeling of excitement and anticipation. Anyone who knows anything about Everest will have heard of the South Col, the last staging post before the summit, and it felt as though today I was going to walk hand in hand with history. I was going to be climbing past and over the famous landmarks immortalised in the many climbing books I had read over the years: the Yellow Band and the Geneva Spur, which guarded the gateway to the South Col.

I was excited and apprehensive. I didn't know what lay ahead but I was ready to confront my fears. I felt strong, ready, and I could feel Everest stirring beneath me.

The sherpas would be arriving soon and would carry some of the oxygen bottles in my tent up to the top camp. I took one of them, attached it to my regulator and put it in my rucksack. A full oxygen bottle weighs about three and a half kilos, so I would be carrying that plus everything that was already in my rucksack.

I opened the tent door to strap my crampons onto my boots. My boots were actually two boots, an inner and an outer boot, as it is warmer that way. I had put my inner boots inside my sleeping bag the previous night to try and keep them warm so I wouldn't be putting my feet into freezing cold boots to start the day.

I looked outside. It was a perfect day; there was a breeze but the sky was clear and it was obviously going to be sunny. I decided it would be warm climbing and I didn't need to wear my down suit, so I packed it away. That took me quite a while because doing anything like that at over 7000 metres is even more exhausting than at Camp Two. I kept having to stop for a rest because my arms got so tired as I stuffed my suit into its bag, and also because I was out of breath. And I wasn't even climbing yet!

My next challenge was going to the loo. I had been putting it off because it meant going outside, putting on my boots, crampons and harness, clipping onto the rope and finding a suitable location that was not in full view of all the other tents. That was a pretty impossible task because there were tents everywhere, but I no longer cared whether anyone saw me with my trousers down because they wouldn't know who I was and I was unlikely to know them.

As I made my way carefully back to the tent, I saw some sherpas I recognised coming up the ropes. The sherpa I was going to climb with on summit day was a young boy called Ang Nuru. He had summited Everest for the first time last year and he was lovely. I think the sherpas are wonderful; in my opinion, they are better than any western guide could ever be on this mountain or any Himalayan mountain because they perform so well at altitude. All the sherpas with our expedition were born at and live at 4000 metres, so they have a head start on us westerners who mostly live at or around sea level.

Because the sherpas live amongst the mountains, they have good mountain sense and I have great respect for them. They know that the mountains can be dangerous, that they can give and that they can take away. The sherpas are almost like a part of the mountains themselves and they understand and they work with them. Because they are used to altitude, they do not struggle at very high altitudes and they are not pushed to the limit like we often are, so they can look after us. They have the spare capacity within themselves to do that. I was very glad that I was going with Ang Nuru. There was no one I would rather be with.

The sherpas greeted me cheerily. They were *always* cheerful, always had a friendly word or greeting for any climber they passed, no matter how heavy the load they were carrying or how they were feeling, because they must get cold and tired too. We can learn a lot from these people.

Ang Nuru checked that I had a full oxygen cylinder in my rucksack and turned it on for me. I put the oxygen mask on my face, clipped into the rope leading higher up the Lhotse face, and started climbing. After about five minutes, I had to pull the mask off my face as I already felt I was suffocating. I had to stop and do that several times before I felt comfortable leaving it on.

I went up the rope, slowly and steadily, feeling more exhilarated the higher I went. After about half an hour, I stopped to catch my breath and looked back down the slope to where I had come from. To my surprise I was a long way ahead of the other climbers who had started off just behind me. I was astonished because I'd thought I was going quite slowly.

I knew my oxygen was supposed to be on a flow rate of 2.5 and I was worried my regulator was turned up too high, so I took off my rucksack to have a look. It was only on a flow of 2.0!

I kept going, putting one foot in front of the other, all the time getting further ahead of the others. I couldn't understand it and stopped several more times to check the flow rate on my regulator, but no – it was somehow just me. My body seemed to be already sensing this was its time.

I could see the famous Yellow Band in front of me, a sandstone rock step about twenty feet high. I knew of it from books, had heard it mentioned so many times in connection with Everest, and now I was actually climbing it. I saw someone in front of me struggling as it is never easy to rock climb in crampons, but I was so used to that from all my years of mountaineering in the Alps that I did not find it difficult.

All the while I was thinking about the climbers who had been there before me: those who had made the first ascent of Everest in 1953, the ones who came after them, and those who had gone up but had never come down. It was as though I was climbing with ghosts, as though there were people helping me, because otherwise how could I be finding it so easy? I couldn't understand it but it felt wonderful.

At the top of the Yellow Band I spoke to Base Camp on the radio to tell them where I was. They were surprised that I was there already – and so was I.

I traversed across to the bottom of the Geneva Spur (the rocky ridge leading to the South Col) and decided to stop there for a drink and to wait for the sherpas. They had stopped for a rest and something to eat at Camp Three and had left later than me, but even so I was surprised they hadn't caught me up yet as they always move quickly.

I took off my rucksack to get out my drink, clipping it to the rope to make sure it didn't fall down the face. The Lhotse face is so steep that anything sliding down it wouldn't stop until it got to the Western Cwm thousands of feet below. The sherpas arrived and rested with me.

I looked at the view. I was now well above the height of Nuptse at 7861 metres, so I knew I didn't have that much further to go to the South Col at 8000 metres. I was excited and pleased that I felt so good. Because I wasn't tired, I was able to enjoy every minute of climbing up this beautiful mountain.

At the top of the Geneva Spur, I heaved myself over the top of the rock face and onto the rim of the famous windswept South Col. I had heard so much about it and had so longed to see it – and there it was in front of me. It was a bleak, desolate place, covered in scree and boulders. Orange and yellow tents were dotted all around with oxygen bottles piled in heaps outside them. Above the South Col was the summit pyramid of Everest, which was – I took a deep breath – much, much steeper than I had imagined it would be. It was also less snowy and much rockier than I had expected. I could trace the route up a steep snow and ice slope, which was broken by rock steps, up to the Balcony, so called because there is a lessening of the angle there for a short way. The South Summit reared up above this. The main summit was further back out of sight, so I couldn't tell how much further it was to the top from the South Summit.

I looked at the route, took it all in and immediately decided not to think about it. I would be climbing up there soon enough, so there was no point in dwelling on whether it looked hard or easy. I would have to take it as it came. There was no going back now.

The sherpas located our tents. I crawled into the doorway of one of them, shoved my rucksack in front of me and sat down to take off my crampons. I had no idea where the others were, but I knew the sherpas were keeping an eye on their progress and they had told me they weren't far behind.

Suddenly Ang Nuru appeared in the tent doorway and said, very strangely, 'Have you been here before Sue?'

I thought this was an odd question, because I was sure he knew that I hadn't and that it was my first time on the mountain. I guessed that he, like me, was trying to understand how I was now climbing so quickly when lower down the mountain I was so slow. 'No, never!' I shook my head and looked at him questioningly.

'You were very quick today. You are very strong, you summit no problem...' And with that, he left.

I sat there, startled. I knew I had been quick. I was surprised how easy I had found the climb up there and was equally amazed – as amazed as the sherpas obviously were – that I had managed to keep up with them. And now I had just received the ultimate compliment from someone I deeply respected and who deeply respected this mountain.

I didn't honestly know what had come over me. The only way I can explain it is that, from the moment I arrived at Base Camp, my body knew it had an immense task before it and subconsciously I had started pacing myself. That would explain why I just could not go fast lower down the mountain: I had been conserving my energy and resources, saving myself for this moment. I had climbed from Camp Two to Camp Three in much the same time as the rest of the team who, up until then, had always been faster than me to the other camps. For some reason, today I had been in another gear altogether.

Even now, as I write this many years later, I can remember how I felt. I can remember my confusion when I realised how quickly I was suddenly moving and being unable to explain it. It felt as though I was suddenly 'in the zone', in the flow. Nothing seemed difficult, not even breathing the thinner air. It was truly the most incredible experience of my life.

I just hoped my body could keep it up for one more very long day because, despite what Ang Nuru had just said, I wasn't at all sure that I would 'summit no problem'. I had absolutely no idea if I would even summit at all! I don't think I had ever doubted I would get this far because I had always felt I would be able to cope with the technical climbing up to this point. Whether my body would have sufficient stamina to get here had been another question. However, here I was and for some unknown reason I still felt strong and not burnt out. But I was nervous – nervously excited.

From here on, I was faced with totally unknown territory in more ways than one. I had no idea how my body would cope with the lack of oxygen at nearly 9000 metres, whether my fingers or toes would freeze, whether I had the physical strength and stamina for the difficulties that lay ahead, and whether or not I would have the strength of mind to overcome the fear of climbing into the unknown, into a place where few women had ever gone before.

I wasn't tired but all the same I took off my down suit, lay down in my sleeping bag and tried to rest. I didn't know what was ahead of me and what reserves I would need.

Vicky arrived with a blast of cold air and threw her rucksack into the tent. It was good to have someone to chat to rather than just have thoughts swirling around in my head. She was as nervous as I was.

The sherpas brought us food and drink. Padawa, the senior sherpa, came into the tent and checked the pressure on the oxygen cylinders we were going to use to make sure they were full. Even though the sherpas perform well at altitude, they also use oxygen on summit day, although they would use only a fraction of the amount that I would.

I thought again about how steep the climb up to the Balcony and the South Summit looked, but reminded myself that there was no point in worrying about it. I put on my oxygen mask and dozed.

67

It was windy and that worried me. I felt so good and I didn't want anything to stop me now. 'Padawa, it's windy. Do you think the weather will be okay?'

'Base Camp weather forecast says that after nine o'clock the wind will drop.'

Well, that was good news! Our weather forecasts, which we paid for, came from the weather centre at Bracknell in Berkshire, England. Hopefully they had got this one right!

I decided I should talk to Base Camp on the radio. Unfortunately that meant getting dressed and booted because I had to go right to the edge of the col and stand on a rock to get a radio signal. From there, I was looking thousands of feet straight down to the Western Cwm.

Communication was a bit crackly but I confirmed with Base Camp that we were each taking four oxygen cylinders, which would be set on a flow of four litres a minute. I wouldn't be carrying all the oxygen cylinders myself; only the one I was using at the time would be in my rucksack. Ang Nuru would carry one for himself and a spare one for me, and the other two were being carried up the mountain by another Sherpa and stashed at the area known as the Balcony. A spare cylinder would be left there for me to collect on the way up, and another spare one for me to collect on the way down. This was the same for every team member.

As I trudged back to the tent, I looked around the col. Tents and oxygen bottles were scattered all around. There were also people walking around from different expeditions. I looked up towards the summit and saw two people coming down the final icy slopes back to the col. Whoever they were, they were very late down.

I didn't like to look too hard at the route we were going to take. It was much steeper and rockier than I had envisaged. I had imagined a trudge up endless snow slopes but the reality could not have been farther from the truth, as I was shortly to find out.

Time passed quickly and soon it was getting dark. We were leaving at nine thirty and would be climbing through the night. I had some last bits of food and a drink, then it was time to get ready. It took about an hour to struggle into my down suit, big boots, harness, head torch, mittens, crampons and ice axe, and by the end of it, I was very breathless … and then I had to find somewhere to put my drink, which I stuffed inside my down suit so it wouldn't freeze.

Finding it difficult to move with everything on, I struggled outside. Ang Nuru was there, packing his rucksack full of oxygen cylinders. He put one into my rucksack, switched it onto flow three and put it on my back.

'My oxygen cylinder should be on flow four!' I protested.

'No, you don't need,' he replied. I couldn't argue. Ang Nuru obviously thought I could manage with a lower flow rate and it did mean that my oxygen would last longer.

I put on my oxygen mask, my hat and my head torch. I wouldn't need my goggles until it was light.

This was it. It felt as though this was the moment I had been waiting for all my life. I was about to climb to the summit of Mount Everest.

Taking the final steps to the summit (Credit Mike Davey)

Summit day
May 15th and 16th

Eventually, about nine thirty, Ang Nuru and I left the others still getting ready and set off across the rocky ground of the South Col to the foot of the summit slopes.

I had never climbed higher than this before and didn't know how I would cope, but I knew my body well from many years of climbing and always listened to its messages. I would be able to tell in the few minutes after we left the tent and walked across the South Col to the start of the climb whether or not I would make it to the summit. If my legs felt tired and depleted of oxygen over that short distance, I knew I would struggle; if they didn't feel tired, I knew I would climb it.

It was difficult walking across the boulders with crampons on, but I felt fine. My legs weren't tired. I had got the message and I knew I would climb this mountain; my body had just told me so.

We walked past a metal pole lying on ground. Ang Nuru stooped to pick it up and handed it to me. It was a big help. Then we hit a long stretch of hard, glassy ice. Ang Nuru reached for my jumar leash and clipped it to himself, making me feel much more secure because there were no fixed ropes yet. When I looked up, all I could see was a long line of head torches above us and I wondered where on earth the fixed ropes were!

After about fifteen minutes, Ang Nuru suddenly stopped, took off his pack, walked over to me, took the head torch off my head and changed the battery. I was astonished – I hadn't even realised it needed changing! After another five minutes we finally reached the foot of the fixed ropes and clipped on our jumars. Here we go, I thought.

We were now in a long line of people. I could see their torches stretching upwards towards the stars. All we could do was keep going with the line. At some points people stopped and we overtook them; at others there was a traffic jam because people were having to climb over rock steps. This was much more exhausting and they had to keep resting.

I found the stop-start very frustrating as it was obvious that Ang Nuru and I could go much faster. The climb up to the Balcony seemed endless. I kept trying to remember how it looked from below, and to work out where we might be on the slope. Eventually, after four hours of climbing, we veered right and I knew we must be coming to the Balcony.

It was now about one thirty in the morning. We negotiated a last steep slope and stepped out of the track. Ang Nuru motioned to me to sit down, which I did thankfully. I took off my pack and changed my oxygen cylinder, leaving the empty one there to collect later. I asked him if he thought we were in front of or behind the others in our team but he didn't know. We were there alone and it felt amazing.

After five minutes rest Ang Nuru said, 'Right, now not too far to summit. I turn your oxygen up to four litres a minute, we go quickly to summit, take photo and quickly descend to col.'

I was in complete agreement. I thought we should get going quickly now in order to stay in front of all the climbers we had overtaken. I looked upwards. It was so steep that I had to crane my neck. I could see a few lights moving above us then merging with the stars. The torches were so high it was hard to tell where the stars began. I didn't feel tired; I felt good and just knew I was going to get to the summit. It was an amazing feeling. The mountain looked so beautiful lit up in the moonlight, which was casting a glow on the snow, the crystals sparkling.

I sensed that the hard part of the climb was now behind us and in front was the South Summit. It was so exciting, so exhilarating, that I kept wanting to jump up and down. I was eager to get going.

The weather was still good. There was no wind but it was cold and I put up the hood of my down suit and wiggled my toes which were also rather cold. Then I realised the problem: the batteries in my expensive boot warmers had run out. I had set the battery to high to warm up my toes when I left the South Col and had meant to turn it down once I was warm, but had completely forgotten about it ... damn! I would have to keep wiggling my toes and hope for the best...

Leaving the Balcony, we walked along what appeared to be a gently sloping narrow track, with drops on either side. For some reason there was no fixed rope here, so Ang Nuru clipped me to himself again – I felt so safe with this boy. The slope steepened. We were completely alone, just me, Ang Nuru and the mountain, which was magical. But as we climbed we came once more to a line of people and again the stop-start began as we climbed more rock steps covered in snow.

The slope steepened even more and became a narrow ridge. I could sense the big drops on either side. I looked to the east; the sky was lightening, and the dawn was arriving. I looked up and could tell there was a peak in front of us. 'Where are we?' I asked Ang Nuru.

'South Summit,' he replied.

I couldn't believe it! I looked at my watch. It was only a quarter to five in the morning. We had been so quick. I looked to the east over Tibet once again and was totally awestruck and emotional. This was more wonderful than anything I could have ever imagined. I was just below the South Summit of Everest with the sun coming up over Tibet, standing on a narrow snow ridge, perched so up high in the sky that I felt I could almost touch the stars.

Suddenly there was the sun, a big red ball, rising over the plains of Tibet. It was so indescribably beautiful. I smiled with my eyes at Ang Nuru and his eyes smiled back. I knew he felt the same way. This was SO truly wonderful.

As the dawn arrived, I finally saw what was in front of me: about four or five people on a narrow snow ridge and, not far above them, the South Summit. In no time it seemed that we were there. The South Summit is a perfect pyramid with no flat place to stand. There were a few empty oxygen bottles to one side where it sloped down steeply to the left, and on the right was a corniced ridge. In front of me I could see the Hillary Step and beyond that a wavy and very corniced ridge. I knew the summit was just along there...

It was truly beautiful and I could have cried for joy. I never expected it to be so wonderful. We dropped down to the other side of the South Summit and had a longer rest while we watched the few people in front of us tackling the Hillary Step, a steep rocky corner. I looked at my watch and knew we were going to be on the summit very early.

And then there I was, at the foot of the famous Hillary Step. I didn't find it too difficult; a few pulls on the rope and I was up. I knew it would be more difficult going back down and it certainly wasn't a place to fall. There were lots of ropes but you couldn't tell the old ones from the new, and the old rope might have been there for fifty years. I just clipped into everything!

At last we were on the wavy corniced crest. I was so excited that tears were stinging my eyes. I knew that at any minute I would see the summit – and then there it was, and I was climbing up the final slopes to the top of Mount Everest.

Ang Nuru looked at me and smiled with sparkling eyes. He stopped and hugged me – yes, we'd done it! A few more steps and we were there on the summit of Mount Everest.

I was so excited, tearful, elated, thrilled that I wanted to jump for joy but Ang Nuru made me sit down. The summit wasn't big enough for jumping around on, and there were drops on either side.

'Please get Base Camp on the radio,' I said. 'I must share this moment with my husband. I would not be here if it were not for him.'

It was seven o'clock in the morning and I was literally on top of the world... Never in my wildest dreams...

Sue talking to Base Camp on the radio from the
summit of Everest

Sue and Ang Nuru on the summit of Everest

Sue in the Western Cwm on her descent from the summit.

PART TWO

HOW TO CLIMB YOUR OWN EVEREST

Discovering the person you were born to be

KEY NUMBER ONE
WHAT IS YOUR LIFE PURPOSE

That's what I wanted to know when I was sitting at home feeling there was something missing, that there must be more to life than this.

1. What is my purpose? What is it that I am supposed to be doing?

I had absolutely no clue how to find the answer to that question and so it came to find me. Big time. My husband died. Wham! That was *not* part of my plan. And suddenly I not only had no idea what I was supposed to be doing but *I had no idea who I even was!* For me, that was the lightbulb moment, the realisation that I didn't actually know who I really was.

2. Who am I really? Who is the person I was born to be?

I was pretty sure I wasn't being the person I was born to be. I felt that if I could discover who that person was, I would know what I was supposed to be doing. That led to the third question...

3. How do I get from where I am now to where I want to be?

That was more of a puzzle. Although I knew where I was at that moment – my husband had just died and I was spinning out of control into a black hole of despair – I had absolutely no idea where I wanted to be. I just wanted to be somewhere other than where I was. How could I get to where I wanted to be when I didn't know where that was?

Luckily for me, my intuition stepped in at that point. Many times in my life I had followed my hunches, my gut feeling and my heart, and doing that had led me to where I was in my life at that moment. Even though it seemed that following my intuition had brought me to a place where I didn't want to be, I couldn't see any other way. My mind felt numb and out of ideas so I decided to follow my heart and listen to my intuition once again.

I set out on a journey of self-discovery to find the answers to those questions:

1. Who is the person I am born to be?

2. What is the life I was born to lead?

3. How do I get from where I am now to where I want to be?

It was as a result of my quest to answer those first two questions that I found myself standing on the highest point on the planet. The answer to the third question was encapsulated in my journey to get there. *How* I got there was by following my heart and listening to my intuition every step of the way. Doing that led me both to my real self, and to the life I was born to lead. It wasn't complicated. Life isn't complicated – unless we make it so.

Your Purpose

1. To discover who you really are and become the person you were born to be.

2. To live the life you were born to lead.

3. To get from where you are now to where you want to be by consciously creating your own reality. In other words by daring to dream and then living that dream.

You have the power within you not only to *unlock* the door behind which your dreams reside, but *to step through it* and start creating the life you have been longing to live. The one you know you were born to lead. *You* have the power within you to do this. You can be exactly where you want to be in every moment – your life is yours to create.

HOW TO BECOME THE PERSON YOU WERE BORN TO BE

It is only if you actually *do* things and have different experiences that you know what you like and don't like, and it is these likes and dislikes that tell you who you really are. That's why, when you feel stuck, you feel like you're in glue; you're literally not getting anywhere and you're not learning anything new about who you really are.

You are presented with challenges because by facing up to and overcoming these challenges you grow, whether it is through challenging relationships, challenging circumstances, or challenges you set yourself. The reason you set yourself challenges and have dreams and goals is because instinctively you know this; instinctively you know when it is time to move forward and grow. Intuitively you are giving yourself a kick up the backside!

So to experience that growth you set yourself a challenge, whether it is learning to sew, learning French, writing a book, losing weight, getting fit or climbing a mountain. It doesn't matter what it is because you will grow hugely in any challenging environment. If you are not challenged, you don't grow and you stay under that nice cosy duvet where it's safe and ... well, pretty boring. But hey, it's safe!

That is exactly why, when you stay in your comfort zone, you feel bored and frustrated as though something is missing. That's what causes that nagging feeling that there must be more to life than this. The reason you feel like you're not getting anywhere is because you're not growing. Instinctively you know that you're not who you think you are. But the question is, *who are you really?*

WHO ARE YOU REALLY?

Not who you think you are! The following anecdote illustrates how, from a very young age, we learn from others to become something we are not.

A friend of mine had a cat which sadly had only three legs. This cat had kittens, all of which had four legs; however, when they started walking around, they copied their mother's movements and only walked using three of their legs. My friend had to teach them to use their fourth leg by tripping them up! In order to regain their balance they instinctively used all their legs, and gradually started walking normally. She said, 'This experience reminded me how to behave around my children. Children are such sponges – they take on your actions and thinking.'

When you are young, the adults in your life are your teachers and you learn by their example. It soon becomes clear from the reaction of the adults around you – parents, friends, teachers – which of your wants and actions are acceptable and which provoke criticism, judgement, anger and the removal or withholding of love, so you tend to modify your actions accordingly. Quite simply, you stop being the person you really are and become someone who fits in with the people who surround you.

At a very early age your mind is trained to tell you not to say or do things that aren't approved of and will lead to love being taken away from you. Those things you learn you must and must not do become deeply rooted in your subconscious mind and grow to become beliefs: limiting beliefs. You have been well trained. They become the 'rules' you live your life by, and you're not allowed to break them … or are you? That is for you to decide. You made the rules of your life; is it now time to start breaking them?

"Your time is limited, so don't waste it living someone else's life. Don't be trapped ... living with the results of other people's thinking.Don't let the noise of others' opinions drown out your own inner voice. And most important, have the courage to follow your heart and intuition.They somehow already know what you truly want to become. Everything else is secondary."

Steve Jobs

KEY NUMBER TWO
DO WHAT YOU LOVE

Following your passion and doing what you love is one of the keys to discovering who you really are.

We all have things we love to do which are unique to each of us. It is when we are doing these things that magic happens. When we are doing something we love, it is like turning the key in a lock and opening the door to our real selves. When our hearts are filled with happiness, when we are feeling inspired, then we are inviting our intuition out to play and saying come and create some magic with me!

It is often when we are doing something creative that we are at our most inspired. That is because we are using our unique gifts and flowing in harmony with who we really are. At those times we are also using the creative part of our brain, which can come up with solutions to anything. It is the part of us where anything is possible and logic goes out of the window.

We all love to do different things. Perhaps for example you love:
Playing a musical instrument
Drawing or painting
Writing
Gardening
Dancing
Walking
Climbing
Cycling
… the list is endless!

Because I love being out of doors in nature, I get some of my most profound insights and inspiration when I am walking in the countryside or gardening. But we are all unique and where you go for your inspiration is likely to be somewhere entirely different.

It's possible that you can't think of anything you really love to do. Maybe you have forgotten some of the things you used to love to do, because life got in the way. Maybe you got married and had a family, or you have a career, or both! You are probably used to putting everyone first but yourself. That is normal and we all do it, but we forget that if *we* aren't happy then those around us won't be happy either.

You are the most important person because if you are happy then everyone around you can feel it. If you are making time to do things that you love, those around you will thank you for it. Happiness rubs off on everyone.

Not long ago I had a client who was feeling lost and stuck and didn't know what she wanted or where she was going. I asked her, 'What do you love to do?'

She said she loved gardening.

'And what else?' I asked.

She couldn't think of anything else. I told her there would definitely be other things she loved to do, perhaps a long time ago, and I urged her to think back through her life.

She sat and thought for a minute, then she said, 'Writing and painting.' She hadn't painted since she was at school thirty-five years ago but she confessed that she still had this longing to paint which she had suppressed because she thought she didn't have time. She had told herself that her family and work must come first. She thought that she had to work to make money in order to be happy, yet she had come to see me because she wasn't happy even though she now had plenty of money...

'So would starting to paint again make you happy?' I asked her.

'Oh yes!' she said. 'Now that you've put the thought into my head, I can't wait to start again. I'm going to order paints and paper the moment we finish this conversation!'

Have you got a gift, a hidden talent, a love for something that you haven't done for many years because you haven't given yourself permission to do it? If so, maybe now is the time to get it out of the cupboard, brush it off and renew your acquaintance with it. By acknowledging and rediscovering these things, you are rediscovering the person who you really are. It is only by doing the things you love and by using your gifts, which are a unique part of yourself, that you will start living the life you were born to lead and being the person you were born to be. Using your gifts will guide you on your path.

That's what happened to me. As you will see, following my heart and pursuing my love of sailing led me to climbing, which in turn led me not only to the summit of Everest but to other amazing experiences. Using your gifts can do the same for you.

We spend a lot of our time doing things we think we should do rather than what we feel is the right thing for us to do, so we are really shooting ourselves in the foot. YOU are the most important person in your life. If you feel good, so does everyone else around you.

We have been taught that putting ourselves first is selfish when in fact it is the most important thing we can do. Even if we have to look after others, there are still ways of doing things that we love. For example, when my husband was very ill I needed to be in the house all day to care for him but I felt such a need to be outside in the hills that I knew my own health would suffer if I did not do something about it.

At that time we were living in the Scottish highlands and the hills were literally outside my back door. It was the middle of summer and we were so far north that it barely got dark at night. I decided to go walking at night while my husband was sleeping. I would get up at two o'clock in the morning and come home five hours later and he did not know I had been gone. Yes, I was tired, but I was happy. It kept me sane and it fed my soul. Because I could do what I loved meant I could give my husband all the love and care he needed, cheerfully and with good grace. If I had not been able to give myself what I needed, I would have been grumpy and resentful at having to stay in the house all day.

We both got we needed. When my husband eventually passed away, I felt no guilt that I had not been there for him because I knew I had been. I was the best person I could be for both of us at that time. I am so thankful that I did that.

No matter what is going on in your life, somehow there will be a way to do at least one thing during the day that makes you feel good, a time when your sole focus is on you. Even if it is just soaking in the bath for twenty minutes, or writing in a journal when you wake up in a morning or just before you go to sleep at night, start making time for the most important person in your life – you! A time when you step into the real you.

EXERCISE

1. In a notebook make a list of those things that really make you feel alive, that make you feel better when you do them. They may not be things that you do any more; they might be things you used to do. Close your eyes and think back to the last time you felt really good, no matter how long ago. Where were you? What were you doing? List at least five things, ten if possible.

2. Rank the things on your list in order of importance to you. Put the thing that makes you feel really good, at number one.

3. Now transfer this list onto the charts on the following pages and create time for a perfect moment at least once every day.

By making this list of everything you love to do, you are starting to build up a picture of who you really are.

MY PERFECT MOMENT

The first week do one activity each day and tick the day you do it. The following week, do two every day, perhaps one in the morning and one in the afternoon. In the third week, see if you can do three, adding one in the evening.

You may think you haven't got time to do more than one but remember that the better you feel, the better your life and that of those around you will be. The happier you are, the more inspired you are and the more productive you will be in your work and home life. You might spend slightly less time sitting at your desk but the chances are that you will find yourself doing better quality work in less time because you feel better. Try it and see!

WEEK ONE

I Love	Mo	Tu	We	Th	Fri	Sat	Su

WEEK TWO

I Love	Mo	Tu	We	Th	Fri	Sat	Su

WEEK THREE

I Love	Mo	Tu	We	Th	Fri	Sat	Su

SURROUND YOURSELF WITH THINGS YOU LOVE

I really love mountains, and if I can't be in the mountains then what inspires me more than anything are *pictures* of beautiful mountains, particularly ones I have climbed or locations I have visited. These are places that mean a lot to me, that literally speak to my heart.

Words are a rather limited form of communication. Everything you see communicates with you on a much deeper level, where no words are necessary. Your body responds to what you see. When you look at pictures, they evoke different feelings in you. I have framed photos of the mountains and places I love on my desk and around my house, so they are with me all the time. I have them in my bathroom so I can see them when I'm brushing my teeth and taking a bath or shower. Simply looking at one of these pictures instantly changes the way I feel and takes me out of my head and back into my heart.

The times you don't feel good will usually be when you are stuck in your head, telling yourself a story about yourself, about things in your life you don't like, about how things haven't gone the way you wanted them to, about the way other people are behaving around you... Thoughts really do affect the way you feel, in the same way as looking at things does! But don't forget you're in charge; you can tell that voice in your head to stop any time you like. You can choose to *think* about something different, something that makes you feel good. If you find that a struggle then find that feel-good place by focusing on things that you love that are physically around you.

It's not just photographs that I have scattered around my house, I have rocks, shells, feathers and other mementos of places I've been and experiences I've had. When my eyes fall upon them it's like revisiting those places and experiences once again. I can remember how amazing I felt because the same feelings bubble up, and in that moment I feel good. I smile! I even get out my magic lamp and give it a rub, because I know that if I dare to dream in that moment, magic may indeed happen...

EXERCISE

1. Create a scrapbook of pictures of things that make you feel good. They don't need to be your own photographs, they can be pictures cut from magazines.

2. Put photographs around your house that remind you of places or things that you love. I stick them on the fridge and on my bedroom door amongst other places.

3. Do the same with objects – rocks, shells, feathers, crystals, anything that means something to you. I have a small rock on my bedside table from a beach that I love and every night before I go to sleep, I hold it in my hand for a moment. It reminds me of that beach and gives me a good feeling to go to sleep with – and who knows what magic I might be creating whilst I sleep! Remember you really are much more powerful than you know.

YOUR GIFTS

Amongst these things that you love to do are your unique gifts. Your unique gifts are an expression of who you really are, that person you were born to be. Using your gifts will lead you towards the life you were born to lead. They will point you to your own personal signposts along the way. The trick is to *notice* the signposts. It is your intuition that draws your attention to them, through gut feeling and those hunches that you have.

You do have more tools in your tool kit than you know … and one particularly powerful one called intuition.

YOU ARE UNIQUE

I'm sure you will have heard people say, 'If I were in your shoes I would do such and such a thing…' That's all well and good, but they are not in your shoes! Even if your shoe size happens to be the same, not only do shoes tend to mould themselves to the shape of your foot but they come in many different designs and colours. Everyone has different tastes, because we are all unique. Life is much the same. There is no 'one size fits all' life.

What works for one person does so because of that person's unique attributes. That's why, when you try to emulate something someone else has done it doesn't usually work for you, for example, copying a business model which has worked well for someone else, or growing your hair long because it looks good on your friend. I did that years ago but it didn't suit the shape of my face, and so I cut it all off again!

Some years ago, I was climbing a mountain in the French Alps with a friend who was an extremely good rock climber. We came to a particularly difficult part of the route, and Graeme told me to watch carefully as he climbed up the rock face to see where he placed his hands and feet so I could do the same.

When it came to my turn, I found myself instinctively doing the moves in a completely different way. I didn't think about it, I just looked at the rock and moved up it, using the holds that felt right for me. Graeme watched in disbelief as I climbed up to him. He didn't believe it was possible to climb the route that way and he made me go back down and repeat it so he could see how I'd done it! Then he went back down and tried to do it my way and he couldn't – he had to do it his way. That was the right way for him.

Whatever you want to do, you have to find *your* way, your path. Even if someone is really successful at something, we can do exactly the same thing in the same way and be *unsuccessful*. We fit our path uniquely but we don't actually know where it is leading us. The only way to find out is to follow our own unique signposts, by doing what *feels right* for us.

That is were the saying 'walk through doors that open but don't try and force doors that are shut' comes from. If something isn't working out for you then follow your intuition, your gut feeling and do it your own unique way. Which is what I did when I was climbing with Graeme. We got the same result and we both got to the top, but by different routes.

Open doors are leading you along your path. That is also what following your feelings will do. They point the way, your unique way.

Your intuition or inner guidance knows the right way for *you* to do things and it will guide you through life if you let it. The key is to get out of your own way and stop trying to do things the way you think you *should* do them. In other words, stop listening to your mind and start listening to your intuition.

YOU MAKE THE RULES OF YOUR OWN LIFE

There are no rules for how you should live your life. The only rules are the ones you make for yourself. No one else knows *you*. No one except you knows what is best for you to eat, to drink, to do or how to live your life. You are in charge of you and no one else is.

Becoming the person you were born to be is about paying much more attention to yourself than you are used to. It is about *taking charge* of your life and your situation instead of *reacting* to life. It is about listening to your body and your feelings, paying attention to how your body reacts to words, thoughts, situations, and learning to decipher what those reactions mean. Do they make you feel good or bad? Everything is a message from your intuition, which is trying to shine a light on who you really are.

When you have to make a decision, how does your body feel when presented with the different choices? You are getting messages the whole time, and it is vital that you start paying attention to how you feel in order to become the expert on you. When you decide to take control and be consciously responsible for all your choices you will find you can guide yourself seamlessly through life.

One day 'experts' say that drinking coffee and red wine is bad for us, the next day they say the opposite. But we are all different and the same foods are not good or bad for all of us. The only way to find out what is right for you is to pay attention to your body and how it feels when you eat or drink something.

I believe that if we could have chosen what to eat when we were very young, we would have grown up eating the things our unique body type needed. We would have got used to asking our body what it wanted to eat. I do that now every day. I ask my inner guide 'What shall I have for lunch? Or dinner? Would I like this? Or would I prefer that?' then I run through the different choices in my mind and see them in my mind's eye. As I do this, I notice how each one feels. One of them will feel better than the others.

It's important to be aware of every decision you make in every moment, to take charge and consciously act instead of reacting, because you are creating your future in this moment. You can't change the past because it's gone, but the future hasn't arrived yet and you are creating it now. Your decisions and actions in this moment define the future and what happens next in your life.

EXERCISE

For the next twenty-four hours, pay attention to how your body feels every time you have to make a decision and are presented with different choices. Run through each possible option in your mind and notice how each one feels. One of the options will feel like the right one. The more you do this the more natural it becomes, until you eventually find yourself doing it with everything. You have been getting messages the whole time, even though you may not have been noticing them!

For example:
1. What should I wear today?
2. What shall I have for breakfast?
3. What shall I do today?
4. Which route shall I take to work?
5. Where shall I go for a walk today?
6. Should I eat/drink this or that?

KEY POINTS
- There are no rules about how to live your life.
- The only rules are the ones you make for yourself.
- The only expert on you is YOU!
- The things you love tell you who you really are.
- We are all uniquely different with unique gifts
- Don't react, take charge of yourself and your life.
- Listen to your body and your feelings.
- The decisions you make now define your future.

"The only really valuable thing is intuition."

Albert Einstein

KEY NUMBER THREE
INTUITION

Think of yourself as something akin to a stereogram. A stereogram is a two-dimensional, computer-generated graphic that has a 3-D image hidden in it. The graphic looks flat on the surface but has hidden dimensions within it, just like we do.

We have a surface-level persona that we show to people. It is who we would like people to think we are and it is often who *we* think we are. But we are much more than that. As with the stereogram, there is a deeper level to our true selves, and it is only by exploring these hidden depths and dimensions that we gradually start to uncover who we *really* are.

One of our hidden dimensions is our intuition. It is not something you can physically see, nor is there scientific proof that it exists. We have to trust ourselves in acknowledging that we are more than our physical body.

I believe that we are all intuitive, and that we have amazing inner vision that allows us to see without using our eyes and to know without using our mind. I believe that we have an inner knowledge that defies logic, which comes from the greater part of ourselves. It is our sixth sense and our own unique inner guide.

It really is your super power! It is the key to living a more expansive, less fearful, go-getting life. Tuning in to your intuition is tuning into your real self not the person you think you are. It is like stepping through a doorway and suddenly discovering you are this person who is much more incredible that you ever thought possible, someone who makes you exclaim 'Wow, is this really me?!'.

YOUR INTUITION IS THE VOICE OF WHO YOU REALLY ARE

The realisation that I was more than my physical body, came to me in the moment my husband died. The only way I can describe the moment of his death is to liken it to a light being turned off. In that split second, I saw his spirit, his energy, leave his body. The light, the energy that had made him who he was, was suddenly gone. All that was left was a physical body that was no longer him.

That moment showed me we are so much more than our physical bodies. For me it was proof that we are spiritual beings having a human experience, that we are energy inhabiting a physical body.

I believe that our intuition is an expression of that energy that makes us who we are and that we are unconsciously guided by our intuition a lot of the time. Our intuition gives us messages in the form of hunches, a gut feeling or simply an inexplicable knowledge that something is right or wrong.

Just before I found out my husband was ill, I had an intuitive knowing about something. The last winter he and I spent in the Alps, we decided we were going to look for a new place to live and I was tasked with the job of finding it. However I never started looking because I had this feeling that it would be the last winter we would ever spend there. I couldn't explain how I knew, I just knew. And sadly I was right. Shortly before the end of the winter ski season we found out that Fred was ill and we went back to Scotland. It did turn out to be our last winter in the Alps and I was very glad I hadn't spent it viewing properties we were never going to live in.

105

Only after Fred died and I had that sudden flash of awareness that I was more than my physical body, did I look back over my life journey and see how I had always followed my intuition without realising it. At crucial points in my life I had listened to my heart, followed my gut feeling and made decisions based on what fel*t* right - as opposed to what my mind told me I should do.

It didn't occur to me that I could consciously create what I wanted until I climbed Mount Everest. In creating and living that dream, I saw how powerful our intuition really is and how powerful *we* are. It was daring to dream and actually living that dream that made me realise we are so much more than we think we are, and that we really can create our own reality and live the life we were born to lead.

I'm sure that, like me, you have had experiences where you've listened to your intuition and done something because you had a feeling about it. So just how aware of your intuition are you? Take the following quiz to find out.

HOW INTUITIVE ARE YOU?

Choose one of these answers for each question.

Rarely = 1 point
Sometimes = 2 points
Often = 3 points

1. I tend to find my own way of doing things rather than doing them the way others say they should be done.

2. I act on my hunches and gut feelings.

3. When I have a decision to make, I can easily distinguish between what my mind is telling me to do and what my intuition is suggesting.

4. I just know when something is the right thing to do.

5. An answer to a question or a problem suddenly comes to me.

6. If something doesn't feel right, I will change my plans.

7. I know things before they happen.

8. I pay attention to how people and situations make me feel, and can sense whether or not they are good for me.

9. I have a lot of coincidences in my life.

10. I pay attention to how my body feels at all times.

11. I regularly take time out during my day to do something that makes me feel good.

12. I am creative and love to play and have fun whenever I can.

13. When I am with another person, I can easily sense how they are feeling.

14. I would describe myself as a happy person.

15. I am willing to take risks and try new things.

16. I look after myself and nourish my body by eating healthily and exercising regularly.

17. I believe my intuition will guide me to the life I am born to lead.

18. I am good at saying no – in other words, I don't say yes when I mean no!

19. I am not afraid to stand out from the crowd and do my own thing.

20. I know that trusting my intuition is the key to living the life of my dreams.

Now add up your points and go to the back of the book to find out how intuitive you are.

WHAT DOES YOUR INTUITION SOUND AND FEEL LIKE?

Most people don't actively use their intuition because they forget it exists, they don't know it exists, or they don't know how to work with it. In particular, they don't know that it can lead them to the most amazing experiences and to the life they were born to lead.

A lot of the time you probably follow your intuition without realising it. If you act on a hunch, or because 'it feels right', congratulations – you're already following your intuition!

Your intuition is your internal GPS. It is talking to you all the time, but unless you are tuned into it you won't hear it. Often even if you do hear it, you will ignore it or you won't trust it and you will listen to your mind instead.

Your mind is a very different kind of voice. For one thing, it never shuts up! Do you find that you have this constant commentary going on in your head about *everything*? Isn't it boring? Your mind just loves to have something to worry about, and the moment you start to feel happy about something it will jump in and say, 'Ah but it won't last...' That is something your intuition would never say.

If you're not sure how to tell the difference between the voice of your intuition and that of your mind, listen up. The voice of your intuition is soft, subtle and never pushy; it suggests and doesn't insist. Intuitive messages come in the form of feelings and emotion as well as in words or pictures in your head. Your intuitive voice is not the voice of fear and would never suggest you harm anyone.

On the other hand, the mind is loud and insistent, demanding that you listen. It is authoritative and will tell you not to listen to your intuitive feelings and hunches because it always wants to be in charge. It wants you to think it knows all the answers even though it doesn't! It's important to turn down the volume of the loud, insistent voice in your head and turn up the volume of that small, subtle voice within which is your intuition and your inner guide.

WHAT *IS* INTUITION?

None of the words we use to describe how we experience our intuition are associated with our head; they have nothing to do with logic or the brain or our mind. They are not *thinking* words, they are *feeling* words, words to do with our senses.

Here are some of the ways we describe how we receive intuitive guidance:

- A gut feeling
- Just a feeling
- Listening to your heart
- Instinct
- A knowing
- Seeing (inner vision)
- A hunch
- Inner Guidance

Dictionary Definitions of Intuition:

- 'The ability to understand something instinctively, without the need for conscious reasoning.'

- 'A thing that one knows or considers likely from instinctive feeling rather than conscious reasoning.'

- 'The ability to acquire knowledge without recourse to conscious reasoning.'

- 'Ability to know or understand through feelings.'

I see intuition like this. What makes us who we are is the energy that inhabits our physical body. However, I believe our energy is so vast that it doesn't all fit into the physical body. The rest of our energy is outside our body, milling around in the ether, the quantum field, or whatever you want to call it. I believe the energy outside our body can 'see' everything – what is happening now, what will happen in the future, and what has happened in the past.

Because that part of ourselves can see what is happening in the future, it gives us messages about that future that feel good or not so good depending on how the outcome looks. We receive feedback via our intuition, which is the messaging interface between the energetic part of ourselves and our physical body. When we *think* about doing something, that greater part of us gives us feedback on whether it would be good or not so good for us. That feedback comes in the form of intuitive hunches, a gut feeling. The trick is to be aware enough to notice both what we are thinking and the feedback from our intuition about what we are thinking. If it doesn't feel good, change that thinking.

Intuition is a powerful tool but so is the mind, if we take charge and don't let it run us. If we can control our thoughts, the words we think and the images we see, then together with our intuition we have the most powerful tools for creating whatever it is we want to have in our lives.

EXERCISE

1. Think of an experience you had when you realised afterwards that your intuition had been speaking to you and you didn't pay attention to it because your mind was so loud. Write it in your notebook so you can see clearly what happened. The more you acknowledge the voice of your intuition, the more you will hear and feel it subtly guiding you.

2. It is important to distinguish between the voice of your mind and the voice of your intuition. They will be different for everybody.

- Write down a list of words that describe what your mind sounds like.

- Next write down a list of words that describe how *your* intuition sounds or feels to you.

KEY POINTS

The voice of your mind:

- Never shuts up! It gives a constant commentary.
- Is a constant worrier.
- Is the voice of fear.
- Is insistent and loud, demanding you listen.
- Is authoritative.
- Recycles your beliefs.
- Tells you what you want to hear.
- It will tell you not to listen to your intuition.

The voice of your intuition:

- Is soft and subtle.
- Is never pushy.
- Suggests and doesn't insist.
- Is expressed through feelings, emotion and images.
- Is not the voice of fear.
- Will never suggest you harm anyone or yourself.
- Is the messaging interface between the greater energetic part of you outside your body that is constantly scanning the future, and the physical part of you experiencing this present reality.

YOUR INTUITION IS YOUR PERSONAL GUIDE ON YOUR LIFE JOURNEY

We've all had intuitive experiences and, whether or not you know it, you will have been guided to this point in your life by your intuition. I know I definitely have, and I will give you a snapshot of my story as an example.

When I was growing up, I loved sailing. My father built my brother and me a sailing dinghy and all I wanted to do was to become a sailing instructor. I left school and decided not to go to university straight away because I wanted to pursue my love of sailing, so I got a job in an office as a secretary to earn enough money to train as a sailing instructor.

One day during my lunch break from work, I met up with my boyfriend who had a friend with him. Over lunch, I asked this friend what he was doing with himself and he said he was at college doing a teaching degree in outdoor education and environmental science. When I asked him what that involved, he told me that as well as learning to teach science in the classroom he was learning to teach outdoor activities, including sailing, climbing, kayaking and skiing. As he talked, all I heard was the word 'sailing'. I could actually do a university degree and learn to teach sailing at the same time? It sounded amazing!

The moment I got back to the office, I picked up the phone and rang that college. It was the summer holidays and not long before the new term would start, so I knew I didn't have much time. At that age I was quite shy; to pick up the phone like that without hesitating was quite something – and quite telling. It really was something my intuition was urging me to do and I was absolutely listening. And that is just the beginning of the story.

When I spoke to the college I was told there was just one place left on the course. I had to go for an interview that week to see whether or not they would accept me. Of course they did! It was just meant to be ... I was following my heart and my intuition.

When I arrived at the college and met the other students, it turned out that many of them were keen rock climbers. One of these climbers became my boyfriend and although I did still sail, my focus moved from sailing to climbing. I fell in love with mountains and became a climber too.

After I finished my degree, my first job was taking people climbing in Britain and the Alps. A few years later I married a mountain guide and moved to live in the Alps permanently.

At every crossroads in my life I followed my heart and my intuition, so it was no coincidence that my husband was not only a climber but a sailor like me. That is how we came to sail across the Atlantic Ocean together on another adventure.

We never know what is around the corner. It is only with hindsight that we can see the bigger picture and see how the pieces of our own personal journey fit together. All we can do in the moment is trust in our heart and our intuition. It will always lead us to where we are meant to be.After my husband died and I spent all that time not knowing what to do, I just knew I had to do *something*. I followed my heart, did what I loved and went back to the mountains, which opened the door to the rest of my life. Your heart and your intuition won't let you down.

EXERCISE

Now it's your turn. Look back on your life, at all its twists and turns, and see how following your intuition and your heart has led you to where you are now. Notice how it has guided you on your journey, even if you didn't realise it at the time.

Don't just see this journey in your mind's eye, write it down. Putting pen to paper is very powerful. By writing down how your intuition has guided you and led you to different opportunities in your life, you are saying to it 'I see you'. You are giving your intuition notice that you are listening to it and intend to work with it to get from where you are now to where you want to be.

FOLLOWING YOUR INTUITIVE GUIDANCE AND CREATING MAGIC IN YOUR LIFE

There are two types of intuitive guidance: conscious and unconscious.

Conscious guidance

I have described in the previous chapter how you can pull your intuition consciously into play whenever you have a decision to make by asking yourself how different choices feel. For example, when you have a choice what to have for dinner, whether or not you should take a particular job, or wear that dress or that T-shirt, your inner guide knows best. When you ask in your head how each of these choices makes you feel, you are actually asking your intuition to guide you. You are awake and alert to intuitive messages, working in partnership with your intuition.

Unconscious guidance

We often instinctively follow our intuitive guidance without realising we are doing it. That is probably what has happened to you on your life journey up to now. It is certainly how I lived my life until I woke up and realised that my intuition was guiding me and that I could work with it to create what I wanted in my life.

Consciously Following Intuitive Guidance

Here are a few examples from my life:

I was planning to sell my house and had decided that June would be a good month to put it on the market. Summer was coming, the garden was looking lovely and I knew that spring and summer are generally thought to be a good time to buy and sell houses.

By the beginning of June I had primed the estate agent, had the photographs taken and the brochure was ready. However, a few days before the house was due to go on the market I was sitting in the garden and thought, 'No, I'm not going to sell my house right now.' It just didn't feel right. I suddenly felt I didn't want to leave that house at that moment. I trusted my feelings and rang the estate agent and told them I wasn't ready to sell, not really able to explain why even to myself!

A few months later in September, I suddenly knew it was time to move. I was certain. I didn't hesitate and put my house on the market straight away. It sold within one week, and within another week I had bought my perfect house in the place I was relocating to. I was in no doubt my intuition had guided me, because if I had put my house on the market in June as planned, the house I eventually bought would not have been for sale.

***

Another example is when I was looking for a life coach to work with. Even though I am a coach, it's always good to keep working on oneself. I found two people I was drawn to and one of them just felt right when I looked at her website and read what she'd written. I sent her an email but before I received a reply I went off to the

Himalaya to lead a trek to Everest Base Camp. Her email arrived while I was trekking and I burst out laughing when I read it. I had told her where I was going and she told me that was a coincidence because her nickname was Everest, a nickname she'd acquired because she had once trekked to Everest Base Camp! Some things are so unbelievable you just can't make them up, and that was definite confirmation for me that I had picked the right coach.

Unconsciously Following Intuitive Guidance

The following examples are times when I was following my intuition instinctively without realising it:

One day I had planned an outing to the coast. The evening before, I was visiting a friend who showed me a beautiful heart-shaped stone that she'd found on a beach. As I was going to the beach the next day, I decided to try and find one for myself.

The following morning, as I walked across the sand taking in its beauty and feeling happy to be there, I randomly picked up shells and stones that I liked and put them in my pocket. I had been walking for about ten minutes when I suddenly remembered that I wanted to find a heart-shaped stone. I searched and searched but couldn't find one. I was really disappointed, as the place I was visiting meant a lot to me; it was somewhere I'd gone for childhood holidays and I wanted something special to take away with me.

When I got home, I put all the stones and shells I'd found on the table. To my astonishment, there in front of me was a heart-shaped stone! It was one of the first ones I'd picked up after I arrived at the beach when I was picking up random stones that I was drawn to, without looking at their shape because I'd forgotten about looking for a heart-shaped one. I needn't have worried; my intuition was doing the job for me all along! Now, whenever I go to any beach I seem to find heart-shaped stones easily and have quite a collection.

**

This next example still gives me goose bumps when I think about it as it seems so incredible. My husband and I were in London together. We both had meetings in different parts of the city, so we arranged a time to meet up at a particular location later in the day. After my meeting I walked to the nearest underground station, deciding which lines I would take to my destination. I would have to change several times and had a choice as to where I would change.

When I have choices, I run through them in my head and usually one will jump out that feels right. I did this as usual, then jumped on the tube, got out, changed tube lines, got on another train and got out again. I walked through a tunnel to the next tube line and stood on the platform waiting for the train. As the train drew into the station, I walked along deciding which door to get in. I stood in front of the door I was drawn to and, when it opened, there in front of me was my husband! We were so startled that neither of us moved or spoke. We were still standing staring at each other as the train doors started to close with me still on the platform and him inside, so he grabbed me and pulled me in.

The chances of that happening? Taking into account different underground lines, stations, trains, doors, not to mention times? Infinitesimal, I would say. Definitely a greater power at work.

And that is not all. When we finally got off the train, in order to recover from an experience that we both found quite overwhelming, we went to a café. There, on the wall behind our table, was a poster advertising the champagne that we had drunk at our wedding. It wasn't a champagne that is normally sold here in the UK. We had brought it back from France with us when we were on a trip over there in the car. Seeing it advertised on a poster in England was astonishing.

Sometimes you really do have experiences that you never forget and that was definitely one of them.

EXERCISE

1. Think back to the times when you were *consciously* guided by your intuition, the times when you actually took notice and acted on your gut feeling and your hunches. Write them all down in your notebook.

2. List the times in your life when you were *unconsciously* guided by your intuition. When did something work out well for you? These will be the times when you were instinctively following your intuition without realising it.

3. Even though your intuition is an intrinsic part of you and not separate from you in any way, it can sometimes help to think of it as your personal guide who has a name. Ask, in your mind, what your guide is called. You will definitely get a reply. You might think the name that appears in your head is just your imagination but it won't be.

4. Once you have asked your intuition what you should call it, talk to it. For example if you call it Rose, talk to Rose. Ask Rose for help with anything: what should you have for dinner tonight; what should you wear this morning; how can you solve this problem? Ask and you'll get the answers.

KEY POINTS

- You really are much more than you think you are.
- You are more than your body.
- You are more than your mind.
- Your body works with you through your feelings.
- You can use your mind and take charge of it, rather than letting it run rings round you. Use your mind as an interface between you and your intuition. When you ask your mind a question, let your intuition answer via your body and how it feels.
- You are an amazing being. When your body, mind and intuition work together, that is a very powerful combination which makes anything possible!
- Miracles do happen.

HOW TO START TRUSTING YOUR INTUITION

This takes trial and error.

You may have walked into situations which, if you had been paying attention to your intuition, you would have known from the start weren't what you wanted. The things that tend to give you the most grief after the event are those things that initially you didn't have a good feeling about but, for one reason or another, you persuaded yourself were a good idea.

It is very important to believe in yourself and what you feel about a situation instead of listening to what others suggest that they would do if they were in your shoes.

I was guilty of that very thing a while ago. I had made a plan to go up a local hill, quite a high one. When I arrived at the parking place and got out of the car I realised it was incredibly windy. 'Hmm, maybe it's too windy,' I thought. 'If it's this windy down here, it will be much windier on the exposed summit ridge'. However, as I looked at the hill I saw there were lots of other people on their way up and that swayed my decision. They obviously thought the conditions were good enough to climb the mountain. Despite the fact that I had reservations, and my over-riding feeling was that this wasn't a great idea, I decided to go because others were going.

I should have known better! The very high winds really buffeted me about, pushing and pulling my rucksack from one side to the other; as a result my back was so stiff the following morning that I couldn't do much for the next few days. If only I had listened to my intuition and not been influenced by what others were doing! After that lesson, I have never made the same mistake again. If my over-riding feeling is don't go, I don't go.

I put this into practice a few weeks later when I was going hill-walking again. Different hill, different location, similar dilemma. This time the dilemma wasn't caused by the weather but by how far I should go. When I got to the summit, I had a choice of routes back to the car. One would take about an hour and a half but the shorter route would only take thirty minutes. I'm used to walking long distances and so my mind was telling me to do the longer route. It was saying that I had only been out walking for a fairly short while and surely I needed more exercise than the short route would give me!

I was literally at a crossroad of paths – which one to take? I did what I usually do when I have this sort of dilemma: I ran both options through my mind to see how each felt.

When I looked at the path which would take me on the long circuit, I just knew I didn't want to do it. I felt tired just thinking about it, so that was an easy decision. My body made it for me, and my decision was confirmed when I felt relaxed and happy the minute I turned downhill on the shorter route. It was so beautiful, with rocky outcrops and wooded glades. I breathed a sigh of relief that I had listened to my intuition.

EXERCISE

1. In your notebook list all the times you can think of when you were pulled two different ways by your mind and your intuition and you listened to your mind. What happened?

2. List all the times when you had a decision to make and you listened to your intuition. How was that experience?

3. I can't stress enough how important it is to recognise the intuitive messages you are getting through your feelings. For some further practise notice the difference in how you feel after answering each of the questions.

- Think of something you really don't like eating.
- Think of something you really DO like eating.
- Think of something you really don't like drinking.
- Think of something you really DO like drinking.
- Think of an activity you really don't like doing.
- Think of an activity you really DO like doing.

Do this with everything in your life, including people you meet, places you visit, shops you go into. How do *they* all make you feel? Practise makes it become second nature, and eventually you will find yourself doing this without thinking about it and living intuitively all the time.

PUT YOUR INTUITION TO WORK!

The more you work with your intuition, the more it will work with you. You will see more synchronicities coming into your life, and you will be more aware and open to your own intuitive nudges, feelings and thoughts. Here are some other ways to put your intuition to work:

In the car

A great time to practise is if you're out in the car and there is a vehicle in front of you. When you get to a junction, ask yourself in your head which way the vehicle is going to turn – right, left or go straight on.

When I do this, I usually get a kind of tingling feeling in either my left or right arm and I am always right about which way the vehicle is going to turn. There was one day recently when I was sure the car in front was going to turn right but to my surprise it turned left. However, as I followed it round to the left it then signalled immediately right and turned into a driveway on the right ... so I put that down as a win!

The other thing I do is consciously work with energy. For example, I am driving along behind a slow-moving vehicle and the road is winding so there is no chance of overtaking it. What I do is harness the vehicle in front in an energy bubble and see and feel it being pulled to one side. Invariably, after a minute or so the vehicle will indicate and turn off the road.

As I keep saying - you are much more powerful than you know. Try these things. Try other things. Experiment! And see what happens. You will surprise yourself.

In conversation

Start using intuitive language. You can change your environment and influence others very subtly by using intuitive language both at work and at home. For example, in conversation or when discussing a decision that needs to be made with someone, use feeling words rather than thinking words:

- My gut feeling says... What does yours say?
- My intuition is telling me that...
- My instinct is to…
- My feeling about this is… How do you feel about it?

When you use the words *feeling* or *feel,* you are speaking from your heart, your intuition, the right side of your brain. The left is the logical side, the right is the creative, intuitive, anything is possible side. If you have a decision to make does it make you feel good/positive/open and expansive or good/negative/closed down? Use this barometer for everything.

At work

At work, use your intuition to help you approach the task in hand. Ask your inner guide for help. Often we really have a struggle with our mind and our ego because we are always striving to impress, to be the best and do our best. We want people to like us. However, we forget that we impress people not by trying to be someone we are not but by being who we really are.

When you speak from your heart and not your head, you speak directly to the other person's heart. They will not consciously realise this is happening; it will happen subconsciously. They will hear you from a different place and be receptive in a different way. They will instinctively start to work more intuitively.

If you speak from ego to ego, you have a more confrontational relationship; you bring in control, with one person saying their way is best and trying to win. Rather than working as a team, everyone is then out for themselves when, more often than not, collaboration works best. On a climbing expedition someone needs to set up the ladders, others carry the equipment, put up the tents or fix the ropes to enable everyone to get to the top. Everyone has different skills and talents that create the desired result when used in combination, a result that may not be reached otherwise.

The word TEAM stands for Together Everyone Achieves More. That can be applied either to a team of people, or to the individual parts of yourself. The individual parts of yourself are your unique gifts, your intuition, your feelings and your imagination. When these parts of yourself are used in combination, they create an unstoppable and powerful force that can pull into physical reality whichever of your dreams and desires you wish to apply them to. You really are a sum of many parts.

"Everything is energy and that's all there is to it.
Match the frequency of the reality you want and
You cannot help but get that reality.
It can be no other way.
This is not philosophy. This is physics."

Albert Einstein

KEY NUMBER FOUR
FEEL GOOD

Feeling good is the most important thing you can do. It is another important tool in your tool kit. So now you have:

- Do what you love - using your unique gifts.
- Intuition - the voice of who you really are.
- Feeling good.

What do we mean by feeling good?

It is different for every one of us, but these are some words that describe that feeling of well-being:

- Relaxed
- Happy
- Peaceful
- Blissful
- Centred
- Content
- In high spirits.

When something makes you feel good it is telling you about who you really are. For me, standing on top of a mountain and seeing beautiful views makes me feel amazing; that is who I am. Understandably, standing on top of a mountain may not make you feel amazing. For you it could be walking on the beach, painting a picture, bungee jumping, swimming ... only you know what makes you feel good.

For example, someone I know absolutely loves watching a certain type of television programme and she finds it hard to understand why I don't. But then again, I love climbing mountains and she doesn't! We are all very different. What makes me feel good is unique to me, and the same goes for you.

Why is it important to feel good?

The only reason we ever want anything is because we believe that in having it we will feel better, feel good, feel happy. But material things often only bring transient happiness because it's not the material thing that we want, it's the feeling that having it brings us. The key is to be able to access the feeling of well-being, of feeling good, without always needing a material thing to make it happen. Feeling good is a state of being. When we feel good we are what we would describe as happy!

When you are happy, you draw more things into your life that make you feel happy. When you're unhappy, you draw more things into your life that make you feel unhappy. Which do you choose?

You are a magnet. Whatever your dominant feeling is, you will attract more of it into your life. If your dominant emotion is discontent, you will attract more things into your life that make you feel that way. If your dominant emotion is feeling happy and full of joy, you will attract more things into your life that make you feel like that. So, if you want to change something in your life right now that you don't like, take your focus off that and instead focus on things that make you feel good!

Here are some examples of things that make *me* feel good:

- A beautiful view
- Being in the garden
- A cup of coffee in my favourite cafe
- Tweed material
- Walking in my favourite places
- Autumn colours
- The smell of roses.

These are all simple pleasures that mostly cost nothing, except the coffee. I love tweed material; if I see it in a photograph or a shop window, it makes me feel good because I love the earthy colours. It reminds me of the hills and the heather moorland, more things that I love.

EXERCISE

Now it's your turn.

You have already listed the things you *do* that make you feel good. This is an expanded list of anything that makes you feel good. This is an 'I Love' list.

In your notebook list all the things you love. When you think you've got to the end of the list, close your eyes for a moment – and then keep going. There will be many more things. They may be things you don't actually have, but just thinking of them makes you feel good. Everything counts. Remember, imagination is everything.

TAKING BACK CONTROL OF YOUR MIND

Imagine if you could permanently access that feeling of well-being whenever you wanted to. You would be able to create the life you want and it would no longer be a struggle.

The key is to recognise what feeling good is actually like and which things, memories or thoughts give you that feeling because it's not just through doing something physical that we get that good feeling, it is in our grasp every single moment through our imagination, thoughts and memories.

We can bring that good feeling into our body and flood it with warmth and happiness whenever we want.

The way to do this is by taking control of the mind. It is very easy for our mind to run rings round us, but we can stop this happening by making our mind work *for* us, give it something to do, something that we want it to do. We can use our mind consciously to put us in that place of good feeling that dreams are made of.

Once you have mastered the technique which I am about to teach you, you will have yet another tool in your tool kit to help you create your heart's desire and bring your dreams into physical reality.

MOMENTS OF BLISS

If you feel good you can immediately access your intuition, your inner guide. It's right there by your side at every moment but, when you're not feeling good and you're stuck in your problems and worries, you don't always recognise it or remember it is there. So how can you feel good even when you don't?

Meditation - but not as you know it...

It's not *how* we meditate, but *why*. The purpose of meditation is to enable us to access a calm, happy and peaceful state of mind at will. Sounds wonderful doesn't it? Sounds easy?

Have you ever tried to meditate but just can't do it? You know it's good for you but:

- You can only sit cross legged for a few minutes.
- You can't sit cross legged at all!
- It's impossible to still and empty your mind.
- Rather emptying, your mind fills up with worries.
- All you can think about is what else you could be or should be doing.

That definitely used to be me. If I sit cross-legged for too long, my knees don't like it. Nor does my mind take well to being told to be still or empty. After five minutes, the voice in my head is telling me to look at my watch because surely the allotted fifteen minutes must be up: 'I have so many things I need to do today!'.

For me the whole experience creates tension and frustration rather than happiness and relaxation and it just doesn't work. It is not surprising that many people try meditation for a while and then give up.

However, knowing that the purpose of meditation is to access feelings of peace and well-being and anchor them within me so they are available at any moment of the day or night, I was determined to find another way of doing it that would *engage* my mind rather than trying to shut it up!

Just as I threw out my personal rule book when it came to climbing Everest, I decided to throw out the meditation rule book and devise a new, simple way to access that wonderful feeling of peace, calm and well-being. The technique is called Moments of Bliss and is so simple that once you have practised it once or twice, you can take it with you and use it in your everyday life. Any time you're feeling sad or stressed, angry or just fed up with life, you can stop for a moment and reach for that moment of bliss. It can change how you feel in an instant; it can take you from a state of sadness, anger or fear to one of happiness, peace and calm. Once you have mastered this simple technique, it really can change your life and the lives of everyone around you because when you feel good, everyone knows it. When you feel good, everything is right with the world.

This technique induces the alpha or happiness state of meditation. Anyone can do it. It can help you to control the thoughts that enter your mind so you can learn to filter them, to banish worries and harsh thoughts in an instant by replacing them with happy ones.

The other good news is that all your happy memories are stored in the same space in your brain so, once you've found that place again, you'll find that other happy memories and feelings you'd forgotten start resurfacing. You'll start smiling more, too! Smiling is contagious; the more you smile the better you feel, and the more you smile at others the better they feel. It's a win-win situation.

This guided meditation will work best if you can record the instructions below on a memo app on your phone and play them back so you don't have to read or remember them as you meditate.

Guided Meditation Instructions

Make yourself comfortable either by sitting in a chair or lying down. I find lying down works well as I can easily completely relax. Make sure you are warm enough and cover yourself with a blanket if necessary.

1. Close your eyes and breathe. Notice your breath. As you breathe in, feel the air being drawn into every part of your body and feel your body relaxing as you breathe out.

2. And breathe.

3. Now move your awareness from your mind to your heart and feel it there. And breathe. Breathe into the warmth of your heart space.

4. And Breathe.

5. With your awareness in your heart, search your memory for a time when you were happy, when you were having fun, a time when you were doing something you loved, something that gives you a feeling of well-being whenever you remember it.

6. What is it that you love – a person, a pet, a special view, a particular place, the smell of fresh flowers, walking on the beach, or simply sitting in the garden with the sun on your face?

Where are you?
What are you doing?

Who are you with?
What are you saying?
What can you hear?
How do you feel?

7. How does it feel to be in that experience? How does it feel to be with that person, to see that view, to smell the flowers? How does it feel to be walking on the beach or sitting in the garden?

8. Capture that blissful feeling and bring it to the whole awareness of your body. You are in that experience again. You have a smile on your face. You can feel how it is to be there. You can feel the happiness, the peace, the contentment. This is your moment of bliss, your place of peace. It is yours to keep and it is always here. Now you know where this place is, you can come here at any time when you want to have a moment of bliss.

9. As you slowly let go of that memory and let it drift away, hold on to that amazing feeling of well-being, of peace, of contentment that you now have. Feel it spreading through your whole body, seeping into every cell, into every space, into every breath, into every part of your being.

10. As you hold on to that blissful feeling of peace and contentment, slowly bring your awareness back to the present moment, back into your body. As you open your eyes, breathe deeply and know that this blissful feeling that you have inside you right now is always there. It is anchored deep within you, within your cellular memory. It

is where your moments of bliss reside. You can go back there at any time.

Now smile ☺

NOTES

It is up to you how long this process takes. Once you know how to do it, and it really is simple, you can put on some quiet music, lie or sit down, access those good memories or images that flood your body with a wonderful feeling of well-being and hold onto that feeling for as long as you want to.

This is the place you want to be as often as you can. It is your key to drawing good things into your life. This is the place where you have instant access to your inner guide, your genie, where you rub your magic lamp and make a wish.

It is your own private place, which you can access at any time you feel down, sad, angry, frustrated, hurt or in pain. Simply close your eyes for a moment and go back to that memory and feeling. Go back to smelling the flowers and sitting in the garden in the sun.

The ultimate key to this experience is to anchor the feeling within you, hold on to it when you open your eyes and take it with you into your day.

Congratulations, you have just mastered the art of meditation!

Living the life you were born to lead

"You can't connect the dots looking forward; you can only connect them looking backwards. So you have to trust ... your gut, destiny, life, karma, whatever – because believing that the dots will connect down the road will give you the confidence to follow your heart."

Steve Jobs

BECOMING YOU

It is one thing rediscovering the person you were born to be, but the important thing is to start *living* as that person and being true to your real self. Once you do that, you are well on the way to living the life you were born to lead.

Here is a review of the important points:

- Your intuition is your guide, but it's vital that you are true to your real self.

- That means appreciating and using the gifts you were born with. They are yours for a reason and by using your gifts, you are appreciating them and acknowledging the person you were born to be. This will open up other avenues for you which will lead you to the life you were born to lead.

- Above all, trust yourself and the way *you* do things. That is the right way. Never mind what anyone else does or says. We're all different and your own way is always the best.

- When you are connected to your intuition, you become connected by that thread to your journey. You start to realise you have *choice* and that you are writing the script of your own life. If your intuition is telling you something, do you want to go along with it or not? Which turning do you want to take – left, right or straight on? These are all choices you have all the time.

- The two most important attributes we have as humans are *free will* and the *ability to feel*. Free will is the freedom to choose, even if it is just choosing a thought which then leads to a feeling which leads to an action. Our ability to feel connects us to our intuition, the greater part of ourselves. Our ability to choose allows us to follow our intuition or not, to choose any path, to choose our thoughts. This is very important, because what we think influences how we feel, which in turn influences how we act.

- It's a simple formula: Think + Feel + Act = Creation.

- You are where you are in your life today because of what has gone before, because of all the good and bad things that have happened to you, because of all the people you've met and the relationships you've had. These are all the result of the choices you've made on your life journey. Up until now, your life journey will most likely have been created unconsciously. You will probably have been working on instinct at every crossroads when you had to choose which way to turn. Now you have the chance to consciously create the next part of your journey. Isn't that exciting?!

144

KEY NUMBER FIVE
DARE TO DREAM

Your journey so far

I want you to take some time now to look back at your own journey. Go back to the exercise in Key Number Three, where you wrote down your life journey, and really connect the dots. Life is a like a giant jigsaw puzzle and it takes a while to fit the pieces together. Look back at your life story and see how you've got to where you are now, and how all the things that were not good in your life at the time led to things that are.

Create a timeline and list the crucial choices you made at the major crossroads in your life. As you do, notice how one thing led to another and that if you hadn't done one of those things, you wouldn't be where you are today.

This is quite a big thing to do. After I climbed Everest, when I looked back over the key choices I had made in my life and saw how they all fitted together and how they pointed me to where I am now, I was blown away. I could see how I had created my own life. However, I also realised that, although I had created it myself, I had done it unconsciously. At the time I hadn't seen that the things I was doing were the steps needed to create what I wanted; I was just instinctively following my intuition.

Once I connected the dots and saw exactly how I had not only dared to dream but created the opportunity to follow and live that dream, I realised I could start to create the rest of my life consciously by following those exact same steps. This was incredibly exciting because it meant I could do or have what I wanted if I put my mind to it. It takes work in the form of focus, intention and energy, but

145

if you really want something you can have it if you are prepared to put your whole self, your whole *being,* into creating it.

The first question to answer is: what do you want?

WHAT DO YOU WANT?

When we are young, we often give up on things we want to do because we are told it's a ridiculous idea. There is no way we could ever be a film star, a rock star, sail the Atlantic or climb Everest because it was not something our parents or teachers could comprehend doing themselves. But they are not you! Parents understandably think they know best, but they only know what they learnt and the rules they were brought up by. They do their very best to guide us and steer us, but in the end only we know what is best for us.

Growing up, we are taught that to get anywhere in life and to get what we want we have to work for it. If we choose the right job and earn enough money, we might be able to afford exactly what we want. But there is another way that involves using your gifts, your intuition and following your heart.

You have spent quite a lot of time learning about, and getting to know, your intuition. This will stand you in good stead. To use a sailing analogy, you have been learning the ropes and how to navigate life using your own internal GPS. You are now about to set sail for uncharted waters and your chosen destination.

Do you know what your destination is? Because that is the first thing you have to decide. Where are you going? What is your goal? What is your dream? Without a specific goal or dream to focus on, you will just drift aimlessly and when you drift you are creating your life unconsciously. In other words, you are pulling into your life whatever you are focusing on and putting emotion into, and those could be things that you don't actually want in your life!

Remember you are a magnet. What you focus your energy on is what you attract into your life. If you are continually focusing your energy on what you *don't* like and what you *don't* want in your life, then you are just pulling in more of the same to it.

Think about it. If your day doesn't start off well, quite often it carries on in the same way simply because you are focusing on those things that haven't gone well. If you can take your focus off those things and refocus on something that makes you feel good, it will change your energy. You will start pulling more things that make you feel good into your day.

If you're feeling grouchy because you stubbed your toe getting out of bed, then tripped over your partner's shoes that were left in the middle of the floor and spilled coffee down your clothes which you had to change so you were late leaving for work, then you got stuck in a traffic jam, and so on, then it's definitely time to change the energy!

While you're stuck in that traffic jam, instead of feeling frustrated and fed up, change your focus. Think of something that makes you feel good – skiing in the mountains, lying on a beach in the sunshine, a pet which you love... Your thoughts and your imagination are creating your life. Instead of letting them run riot, take charge and use them to create the life you want.

So what do you want?

What If I Don't Know What I Want?

Many years ago, when I set out on this journey of self-discovery, I read a lot about how to make dreams and desires come true. But what if you don't have a dream and you don't know what you want? Not everyone does. A lot of the time, what goes on in your head is a mish-mash of different thoughts and ideas that crash and collide whilst you get on with your daily life.

Often the reason you don't know what you want or don't have a dream is because you are too focused on the things in your life that you don't like. These things are taking up all the space and mental energy, leaving no room for anything else. To bring everything you want in your life into focus, it can help to first highlight everything that is in your life that you don't want.

EXERCISE

1. In your notebook, at the top of a page, write *Things I have in my life that I DON'T want.* List everything that is in your life right now that you don't want, the things you don't like and complain about. Get them out of your head and onto the paper.

Writing them will bring clarity to muddy waters. It may be a very long list and putting these things down on paper will illustrate how much mental space they have been taking up. Clearing out the clutter of your mind makes space for new things to appear, new ideas, dreams that have been hiding at the back of the wardrobe of your mind, put there long ago and forgotten about.

2. Now you are clear on what you don't want in your life, it should be easier to write the list headed *Things I have in my life that I DO want*. List everything that is in your life right now that you do want and what you like about it.

3. The final list is headed *What I really want!* This is the magic list where you will write down all the things that aren't in your life right now but that you would like to be. This is where you start to create your future.

Do not limit yourself here, because these things are your dreams. What would you like to do? What would you like to have? Where would you like to be? Who would you like to be with? It doesn't matter that you have no idea how you could possibly have these things and that they seem completely out of reach, write them down! Get them out of your head and put them onto paper. That's how you reach your goal – by starting. Writing it down makes it real.

Allow yourself to daydream about possibilities. By doing this and deciding what you want, you are acknowledging the real you, not the person you've become. Your *real* goals and dreams, your deepest desires, are not things that anyone else wants for you; they are yours and yours alone.

4. Now put the things on your *What I really want* list in order of importance. Which one do you *really* want? Focus on the one thing that you really want to create. You must have total clarity. Be clear. What is your dream, your goal, your Everest? Don't let that voice in your head tell you that it is impossible. Don't let it make you move what you really want down the list, because I know from

experience that when you're on the right path seemingly impossible obstacles simply melt away. It is true that you can move mountains. Illusory mountains can seem very real when they are blocking the path to your hopes and dreams, but you are so much more powerful than you think. If you use the tools in your tool kit and let your intuition guide you, nothing can get in your way.

Do you want this dream with all your heart or with all your mind?

There is a big difference between desiring something with all your heart and desiring it with all your mind. The latter is ego driven – in other words, you want to achieve whatever it is in order to be better than, or more than, other people, or to prove something to other people.

If your desire is ego driven, this process will not work for you because you are trying to make something happen that is not in alignment with who you really are. This process of achieving your dream is all about following your heart and your intuition, your unique personal guidance system. It is driven by the heart-mind, not the ego-mind, so be clear about why you want what you want. Be true to your self.

KEY POINTS
- Be clear.
- What do you want?
- Why do you want it?
- Do you want this dream with all your heart?
- Aim high.
- You can move mountains.

"Nothing is impossible.
The word itself says 'I'm possible'."

Audrey Hepburn

KEY NUMBER SIX
FOLLOW YOUR DREAM

Now you have dared to dream and identified your goal, the next step is to follow that dream and create the opportunity to actually live it. Taking my own journey as an example, once I had decided I really wanted to climb Everest my next challenge was to create the opportunity to climb it. Unless I could get myself to the bottom of the mountain, to Base Camp, then I would never have the chance to try and climb it.

Using the Power of your Imagination

Your imagination is another powerful tool in your tool kit. As I have stressed, clarity is everything and it is very important to make sure your goal isn't fuzzy. You might think you know exactly what you want but, if it's still an idea in your head or a sentence on a page, the chances are that precisely what you want is still unclear.

You might decide your goal is to move house. You have an idea of where you want to move to and what sort of house you want, but if you want your dream house in the perfect location then the more precise you are about what you want, the more likely you are to attain it. So your next task is to write about what it is you want in detail. Writing it down makes it real. By re-writing your life as you want it, you are re-wiring your brain.

EXERCISE

1. Describe every aspect of what it is you want in the present tense. Imagine you are already living that dream and are telling someone about it. For example, you might write, 'My new house is in .... (insert location), surrounded by beautiful countryside, with wonderful views from all the windows...' and so on. Describe all the rooms in detail, as though you are actually living there now and can see it.

2. Next, describe your new life at that house. Who are your friends? What are your neighbours like? If you have children, where do they go to school? Imagine how you see it unfolding, play make believe, daydream.

If it's a new job or career that you want, describe what it is you want to do. Where do you work, how do you get there? Describe your day as though you are actually doing that job. Use the power of your imagination. What are you wearing, what is your boss like and your co-workers? Or are you the boss? How does that feel?

3. The next thing is to describe how having what you want makes you feel! How does it feel to be living in your new house or working in your new job? How does it feel now that you've lost weight or got fit enough to climb that hill? Whatever it is, see it in your imagination, *be it*. Feel how it feels and put that into words as best you can, then add in things from your other senses. What can you smell? What can you hear? You are writing the story of your future life ... so make it as good as it can be! No holds barred. Remember to aim high....

4. Read out loud and record what you have just written. For this, I use the memo app on my phone. When you have recorded it, play it back over and over whenever you can. When I am in the process of creation, I play my recording on a loop in the car when I'm driving.

Immerse yourself in your dream. Live it, listen to it, see it in your imagination, feel it, taste it, be it as often as you can. You have to focus all your energy on it and believe me, it will be worth it. As I have said, do not underestimate your power of creation. Once you understand how to use all the tools you have at your disposal, you are an unstoppable force.

THE SECRET KEY

When I dared to dream and knew I wanted to climb Everest, I had no idea how to go about it. Without realising what I was doing, I asked myself the question that was the secret key to unlocking the door behind which my dream resided...

Once I had answered that question, opened the door and stepped through it, I knew exactly what to do next. From that moment one step led to the next step, and one miracle seemed to lead to another miracle, until there I was at Base Camp, face to face with my mountain!

The secret key is a specific question that connects you to your inner guide because it allows you step into your future without limitation or boundaries. It is saying 'let's play make believe' or 'what if...?'.

The key question I asked myself is: 'If I were going to climb Everest, what is the next thing I would do?'

Asking this question immediately takes you out of your head and into your heart. You are speaking directly to your intuition, to your inner guide, to the greater part of yourself.

Simply insert whatever your dream is in that sentence, and see what answer you come up with!

The answer when I asked that question was that my next step would be to climb another big mountain to see if my body could cope with the lack of oxygen at high altitude, and to find out if I had the mental strength for such a big challenge. If I didn't make the grade with both of those tests, there was no point in trying to get the money together to climb Everest.

EXERCISE

1. Ask the question: 'If I were going to ... what is the next thing I would do?'

2. Take the step you are directed to take, and trust that once you have taken one step you will be led to the next. There will be signposts which come via your intuition. If you can't see a signpost, it is because your mind is in the way – you are getting in your own way. Perhaps you don't want to take that first step because it feels like such a risk, even though your dream is on the other side of it.

Leaving the safety of your comfort zone

'Take the step you are directed to take...' Sounds easy, huh? However, no matter what your goal or dream is, it will inevitably involve changing your life in some way. It's all very well having dreams, but having them come true means stepping outside your comfort zone. It means you have to come out from under the duvet.

Change can feel scary. We are programmed to need to know the outcome; if we don't, we want to stay in our comfort zone. Anything new and different tends to make us feel fearful because it is not familiar, but eventually the new and different become part of your routine and your new comfort zone. That is how you grow and move forward in your life.

Once you start moving towards something you haven't experienced before, you may feel fearful because you believe you have no control over the outcome and you are desperate for it to turn out well. But you have more control that you think. You have tools in your tool kit that have always been there that you can use to help you to determine the outcome.

I will tell you once again – you are much more powerful than you know. Look how you have created your life up until now! Imagine how amazing your life can be if you actually do this consciously and create what you want! Yes, you will still have some things in your life that you don't want, but they are there for two reasons.

- You created them unconsciously and pulled them into your life through the thoughts you were thinking and the emotions you were feeling. Imagine yourself as a giant radio transmitter and receiver. When it is tuned to a certain frequency or channel, it will *receive* whatever is on that channel. If, for example, you are tuned to and transmitting anger and frustration, that is what you will also receive. It works exactly the same for joy and happiness … if you are tuned to that frequency, you will receive more of the same. Whether you are happy or sad, angry or joyful, everyone around you can feel the emotional frequency you are emitting. That is why, if you are a happy, positive person, people who are angry and sad are hard to be around because you literally aren't on the same wavelength.

- We need contrast in our life. If you don't have things in your life that you don't want, how can you know what you *do* want? Perhaps you weren't sure whether or not you wanted something so you chose to try it. If it didn't turn out well then you learnt more about what you *do* want in your life, so next time you can make a different choice.

So do you want to live your dream or stay in the rut you're in? We are very good at persuading ourselves that we are happy when we're not because we are afraid of change. It's not easy to take that step through the door towards your dream. I know, because I have done it many times, but each time it has been worth it.

If you are at a crossroads and aren't certain which direction you are being guided to go, run through each of the choices in your head and see how each one feels. The one that feels the best choice is the signpost you are being guided to follow.

Even if you aren't certain it's the right choice, taking any decision is better than staying in the same place and waiting for the world to come to you. If you move forward in your chosen direction, even if it's not very far, everything will start to become clearer. Small steps still get you to where you're going. The most important thing is to begin.

Don't forget you are a magnet. Hold your dream in your heart, take a step towards it and your dream will start coming towards you.

MEDITATION
Meeting Your Future Self

This is another tool in your tool kit. You have already described your dream in detail by writing it down, recording it and listening back to it. As you did this, you will have imagined living your dream. You know what it looks like. This meditation takes that one step further; you are stepping outside time and going to meet your future self who is living that dream now.

You need to suspend all rules, limitations, beliefs and judgment and imagine. When you are immersed in your imagination, you are outside time in that place where anything and everything is possible.

- Imagine there is no such thing as time.

- Imagine that past present and future don't exist separately, but that they are all happening right now in the quantum field.

- Imagine that there are infinite versions of yourself and that every choice you have had at every crossroads in your life is being experienced by a different version of you. All possibilities exist, all endings exist; which one you experience depends on the choices you make.

- Imagine that your dream is already being experienced by one version of your self. This meditation is going to take you to meet that version of you so you can ask her or him for help in achieving your goal.

I would suggest that you record this meditation so you can play it back to yourself. For this meditation, which is broken into time segments, I use a timer app on my phone set for five-minute intervals.

Meditation technique

This meditation is broken into segments of five minutes, so set your timer for four five-minute intervals.

- The first five minutes is about getting comfortable enough to be still for the next fifteen minutes – it's wiggle and fidget time!

- The second five minutes is about engaging the mind positively. You are in control and it's all about feeling good and charging up your body with that wonderful feeling of well-being, happiness and contentment that is available to you.

- In the third five minutes you are stepping outside time to meet your future self – the version of you that is already living your dream. This is the space where you can ask your future self advice about how to get to where she or he is now.

- In the fourth five minutes you leave your future self and step back into your present reality, bringing with you everything you have just seen or heard.

Guided meditation instructions

First five minutes
1. Close your eyes and get comfortable.
2. Wiggle around if you need to.
3. Gradually start to relax your body by clenching and relaxing your fingers. Do the same with your toes.
4. Consciously unclench your jaw by opening and closing your mouth.
5. Take a few deep breaths and feel your breathing slowing down.
6. As you do so your mind will gradually also slow down and stop whirling so much. Now is the time to let it all out and let it all go.

Second five minutes
1. Consciously take your awareness from your mind to your heart.
2. Now bring into that awareness everything you can think of that you love. It may be a particular person, a pet, a special view, or a particular place.
3. Spend the next few minutes seeing the images of everything you love pass through your mind and with every image feel the feelings of love, well-being and contentment that they give you. Let that feeling flow through your body and fill you up until you are overflowing.
4. Capture that feeling and feel it seep into every part of your being.

Third five minutes
1. As you slowly let those beautiful memories drift away, hold on to that feeling and anchor it within you.

2. Now bring your dream, the goal you so dearly wish to achieve, into your awareness

3. Imagine yourself living this dream. Think of it as a movie in which you are playing the central role. What are you doing? What do you look like? What is around you? What can you see, hear and smell? Who else is there? How do you *feel?* Imagine it in as much detail as you can.

4. *Talk* to the person who is playing you in this movie. Ask whatever questions you might have about how they got to live that dream. How did they get to where they are now? They have already taken the journey from where you are now to where you want to be, so they are in the perfect place to advise you. They may give you the answers to your questions right now, or the answers may come later.

Fourth five minutes

1. Say goodbye to your future self for now. Let all the images dissipate and lie quietly. For the next few minutes just be still and see what comes to you; you may get other images or words coming into your mind, you may even get answers to the questions you asked the future version of your self. Even if you get nothing, that is perfect too: there is no right or wrong.

2. As you sense the five minutes coming to an end, or when you feel ready, gradually start to move your fingers and toes, and bring your senses back to the here and now. When you are ready, open your eyes and merge once again with your present reality.

3. Treat yourself gently for the next few minutes while you get ready to carry on with your day.

Smile!

NOTE

Whilst you are in the process of creating your dream and bringing it into this reality, I would recommend doing this meditation every day. The same goes for listening to the recorded description of your dream. The more you immerse yourself in this process, the more evident the next steps to take will be and the quicker and more easily your dream will become your present reality.

"Go confidently in the direction of your dreams. Live the life you have imagined."

Henry David Thoreau

KEY NUMBER SEVEN
LIVING YOUR DREAM

Mastering The Art Of Creation

Up until now you have been training to climb your Everest, learning all the different skills necessary to help you reach the summit and attain your dream. You have been learning to use the tools you already have within you to master the art of creation. Now it is time to start creating and putting that art into practice.

Imagine you are training to be an artist. You have learnt drawing skills, how to mix paint colours and you have practised different painting techniques. Now it is time to paint your first picture, the picture you have been dreaming of painting all through your training. This is what you are doing as you set out on your journey and start pulling your dream into reality. You are painting the picture of the life you really want and living it as you paint it.

The art of creation is what life is all about. It's where you start to grow and to learn about who you really are. Each step forward is a new challenge overcome, and in overcoming each challenge you learn something new about yourself. You begin to understand your life purpose. You grow into the person you were born to be and start living the life you were born to lead.

So as you trek towards your base camp and the mountain you are about to climb, let's take a moment to review the steps that make up the art of creation.

- **Decide** what you want.

- **Feel Good!** Focus on feeling good by mastering your thoughts.

- **Imagine** living your dream whilst anchoring those good feelings.

- **Ask yourself the key question**: 'IF I was going to…' then listen to your intuition.

- **Take some physical action**. Follow your intuition and step towards your goal.

- **Keep following the signposts.** Remember how you created your life unconsciously up to this point? Now you are *consciously* creating your life. Doing it on purpose! Now you know what to look for, your intuition will place signposts at every crossroads you come to. Which way you go is for you to choose.

BASE CAMP
The importance of the journey

It is never wise to go straight from Base Camp to the summit because it is on the journey that most of the learning takes place. Your goal, your dream is simply the vehicle for that learning and growing to happen.

Whatever your goal, the journey is just as important – if not more so – than the end result. The climb towards your goal shapes your character, offers you opportunities to grow and tests you to see how much you want to get there. It is during the journey that you learn about yourself and the greatness that inhabits you. You get to develop the *qualities* of greatness, like perseverance and courage, resilience and patience.

The moment of actually achieving your dream feels amazing, but it is purely that – a moment in time. It doesn't bring you the same gifts as the journey to that dream does.

We learn more from the times that test us than we do from times of success. I learned more from the drudgery and the danger of going up and down the mountain acclimatising than I did from actually standing on the summit of Everest.

It was on the way up the mountain, that I learnt the things that not only helped me to grow, but that I have been able apply to so many other aspects of my life since then. The lessons I learned, the life secrets, are the things I am sharing with you here, so that you too can not only dare to dream, but begin to make your dreams a reality.

CAMP ONE
There is no hiding from who you really are

The whole point of this journey is to discover who you really are. As you start to climb your mountain and move towards your goal, you will find that you naturally start to break through your self-imposed limitations and throw away your rule book of life because it is the only way forward. You cannot bring your dream into reality within the strictures of limitation and boundary. Dreams do not exist in that place. The person you really are, knows only unlimited expansion, and there will come a point when it becomes apparent to everyone around you that you are not the person they thought you were.

It was because I had thrown *my* rule book out of a plane window that one day I found myself sitting in a tent at Everest Base Camp telling my husband that I was not the woman he thought I was! I could no longer be the woman who made herself out to be as strong as all the male climbers. I was technically as capable yes, but as strong – no! For the first time in my life I was having to admit to myself – and my husband – that I could not carry as much in my rucksack as the men on the expedition. I needed help. For me, this was a very big deal.

I have been a climber all my adult life, and when I started climbing many years ago I was most definitely a woman in a man's world. In those days, female climbers were in the minority. In order to be accepted, I always felt I had to be seen to be as good and as strong as the men. It wasn't easy, but I had managed to fool both them and myself! Now I was having to admit that I was wrong.

This confession was precipitated by the fact that I struggled to carry all my equipment on the various forays up the icefall to Camps One and Two – sleeping bag, sleeping mat, warm clothing, food, stove, water and more. I managed but I found it exhausting and I knew it was draining me physically. I knew that if I didn't ask for help to carry my equipment, I would not make it to the summit. There was no way I was going to let my ego stop me reaching the top of this mountain.

Of course, my mind was telling me not to be ridiculous but my intuition was telling me otherwise. I had got this far by listening to that quiet voice so I wasn't about to stop now.

Even though asking for help was a very difficult thing for me to do, I looked my husband in the eye and told him I was going to ask a sherpa to help me carry some of my equipment. My husband didn't like it! I had never shown this side of myself to him before. He was angry; in his eyes, asking for help made his wife appear weaker than the rest of the team. I didn't care and I stood my ground. I knew that by saying out loud that I was not as physically strong as the men made me stronger, not weaker. It gave me confidence that I could make the correct decisions for my body so it could pace itself through the long expedition.

I was starting to discover who I really was. Rather than feeling disappointed in myself for asking for help, I felt proud for doing so. Having admitted my 'weakness', I finally felt free. I was going to be me, whether the world liked it or not!

CAMP TWO
Don't rush, pace yourself

Not only had I been trying to prove I was as strong as the men by carrying as much as them, I had also been competing with them. They climbed faster than me and I always trailed into camp last. At first I tried to keep up and pushed myself too hard, but I felt lousy and I knew inside that it was the wrong thing to do.

The same day that I stood up and said, 'I'm a woman and I can't physically carry such a heavy rucksack,' I also decided I would go at my own pace. So what if I arrived at camp last? I was no longer going to worry about it.

I decided to plough my own furrow. I had decided to be me and that was who I was going to be. We are all different and we aren't meant to do things in the same way. Even though we were all climbing the same mountain, we didn't have to do it at the same speed or in exactly the same way.

This goes for whatever you are trying to achieve, whatever your Everest is. We have to find our own way to climb our mountain. Look inside yourself and do it in the way that feels right for you.

Take time to breathe and reassess your position at every stage on your journey, at every camp on the way up the mountain. Stay at each camp for a while and acclimatise. Survey your surroundings, assimilate what you have learnt up to that point, then feel for the next signpost. And when you feel ready, move up to the next camp.

CAMP THREE
Letting go

You can't actually see the summit of Mount Everest from Base Camp. It wasn't until I was higher up the mountain that I finally saw the route I would be taking from the South Col to the top. It looked so far that my first thought was that I couldn't do it.

I felt daunted and questioned why I was there. Who was I to think I could climb the highest mountain in the world? I don't think many people actually thought I could, which was why I had told very few people that I was coming to Everest. I didn't want to be judged or to see their looks of surprise. I knew they would be thinking I had bitten off more than I could chew. I was a climber, yes, but not one anyone had ever heard of. I was just the girl next door.

Yet I had got this far. I had followed my heart, my gut feeling, all the way here; surely, in that case, it was meant to be? Since the day I had admitted I needed help carrying my equipment, I had become quite good at shutting out the voice of my mind.

In fact, Ang Nuru, the sherpa who came with me to the summit, had gladly offered his help and told me it was a good idea. He agreed that I should conserve my energy lower down the mountain because I would need everything I had later. Every single mental and physical reserve would be called upon.

As I sat and looked at the summit, any confidence I had ebbed away. In its place I felt fear seeping in and with it the voice of my mind. No matter what I told myself about all the long mountain days I'd had in the alps and all the hard climbs I had done, it didn't change the facts: it was a very long way to the summit and it was very high up there. I wouldn't be *in* the clouds, I would be high above them. Planes would be flying *below* me. I would be nearer to space than the sea; space starts at 12,000 metres and I would be at almost 9000 metres. I had no idea what would happen to me. I could very possibly die...

As my mind droned on, making me feel worse and worse, I suddenly snapped out of it. I suddenly knew what I had to do: I had to let go of my goal and stop thinking about the summit because it was that which was scaring me. I decided I wouldn't look up there any more, I would just think about what I was doing right here, right now, and what my goal was for *today*.

From that moment on, I decided to literally take it one step at a time. Thinking in that way suddenly made the whole thing seem easier and less daunting. I broke the main goal down into smaller ones, ones which I knew I could achieve. I knew I could get to Camp Two, and after Camp Two my goal was Camp Three and then Camp Four. If I got that far then maybe, just maybe, I would be ready to go for the summit.

Once I had made this decision, I started to feel much better. I was more mentally prepared, and as a result my confidence returned. When I had reached one camp, I would rest, relax and then start focusing again, not on the summit but on where I was going next.

By doing this, when I finally reached the top camp at the South Col I was as prepared as I ever would be for what I knew would be the hardest day of my life. I was calm. I had already overcome so much. The way in which I had coped with the day to the South Col, when I suddenly felt as though I were breathing rocket fuel rather than oxygen, had given me confidence. I was completely focused and I was in the zone. I had no idea whether or not I *could* reach the summit or what would happen to me on the climb up there, but I knew the only way to find out was to try.

Any goal can seem hugely daunting when you first realise what you have taken on and how hard it might be. At that point, fear and the voice of your mind can step in. If you're not careful they can take over and, before you know it, you are back down the mountain where you started, treading water in your uncomfortable comfort zone. So take pre-emptive action!

Take your focus off the summit; let go of the goal and focus on the now. Zoom out of the big picture and zoom in on the minutiae. Break the main goal down into smaller ones that aren't so daunting, ones you know you can accomplish. Your confidence will grow with each small goal you achieve, together with your knowledge and your skillset. By letting go of the main goal and focusing on the next step, you are preparing yourself gradually for summit day.

If you do this, you will be at the top camp before you know it. You will be so well prepared, so focused, that taking those last steps to your goal will seem easy. You will take them in your stride and wonder why you ever doubted yourself. In that sublime moment of achievement, you will realise that, if you can do this, you can do anything. Dreams do come true and, in achieving this, you have found what you were always looking for: yourself.

CAMP FOUR
Mental strength

We all have challenges we want to overcome and dreams we aspire to, but it is natural to have doubts when you want something really badly. You may well be surrounded by others who not only doubt you but who also voice those doubts. That is why it is so important to have the mental strength to keep going when everyone around you is expressing their doubts. You need the strength to follow your heart and your intuition, to shut out the voice in your head that says the risk is too great and you should turn around.

You have already proved you have this strength within you because you would not have got this far without it. It takes great will power and mental strength to follow your dream because you are stepping outside life's boundaries. You are challenging the limitations that have been set for you by others and that you have set for yourself, and you are challenging the beliefs that go with them. That is the mark of greatness, the mark of someone determined to become the person they were born to be. It is the mark of someone who has decided that stepping into the unknown is a risk is worth taking because that is where true freedom lies.

'To laugh is to risk appearing the fool, to weep is to risk appearing sentimental, to reach out for another is to risk exposing your true self. To place your ideas, your dreams before the crowd is to risk their loss, to love is to risk not being loved in return, to live is to risk dying, to hope is to risk despair. To try is to risk failure, but the risk must be taken, because the greatest hazard in life is to risk nothing. The person who risks nothing, does nothing, is nothing. He may avoid suffering, but he simply cannot learn, feel, change, grow, love, live. Chained by his certitudes, he is a slave. He has forfeited freedom. Only a person who risks is free.'

William Arthur Ward

REACHING THE SUMMIT
We all need a sherpa in our lives

Knowing that you are not facing this challenge alone, and having someone on your journey to light the way ahead, guide you, believe in you and to encourage you, can be the one thing that you need to get you to the summit of your own Everest.

Before I climbed Everest, I was newly widowed and in a deep spiral of despair. I felt lost and alone, unable to see a way out of the dark tunnel I had found myself in. It never occurred to me that it would be useful to have someone who could guide me through the darkness to the light. Growing up, my experience of life had been that you battle through life's challenges alone. You grit your teeth, bear it and don't ask for help. My experience of Everest changed all that.

I didn't climb to the summit of Mount Everest alone; I had a coach, a guide, with me in the guise of Ang Nuru. He is someone who lives in the shadow of Mount Everest, who understands and respects the mountain and who knows, lives and breathes it. He possessed all the qualities of a perfect life coach; he not only showed me the way but, more importantly, he gave me the belief and encouragement to trust that I had the necessary qualities within me to fulfil my dream.

We all need a sherpa in our lives, someone who believes in us when we doubt, who supports and encourages us when our will is weak. Just like a life coach, my sherpa recognised qualities in me that I didn't see. He recognised me as someone who could reach the top, even though I couldn't see it in myself. We can be 95% fit for a task but we are often afraid of taking the last few steps towards our goal, either because there is risk involved or we lack belief in ourselves. Having someone there with us to hold our hand and be there with us, helps us take that final step towards our dream because we are not doing it alone.

We still have to make all the moves and take the final steps to the summit ourselves, but having someone along on the journey gives us courage, someone who knows the goal can be achieved not only because they see it in us but because they have been there before us. They know that if they can do it, so can we because they know that if we can dream it we can achieve it.

The sherpa who stood on the summit of Mount Everest with me knew how hard it was because he had climbed it before, but he knew I could do it because he had seen it in me. I was the one who doubted and lacked belief in myself.

Your cheerleader can be a supportive friend or partner, a life coach or a mentor, someone who's been there, done it already and can guide you along the path you are travelling. Your way won't be the same as theirs but, because they have made that journey themselves, they will understand the steps involved and the challenges you may come across on the way.

I had a coach and mentor long before I decided to climb Everest even though I didn't know it at the time. It only occurred to me afterwards that all the years of mountaineering and ski touring in the Alps with my late husband, Fred, had been the perfect preparation for this challenge. It was Fred who had taught me how to pace myself during long mountain days.

We have coaches and mentors by our side at all stages of our life, even though we don't always realise it. We are not meant to struggle through life alone and it isn't a sign of weakness to ask for help. My experience taught me that when you work together with other people it can catapult you to levels of achievement that you would never have believed possible. Why settle for mediocrity when you can have the best, the biggest or the highest? Remember, the danger is not in aiming too high but in aiming too low and achieving it.

Dream big, because big dreams really do come true...

EPILOGUE

If you always do what *feels* right, you will always get to where you want to be. On the way you will have adventures, there will quite possibly be miracles and I'm sure there will be magic. Enjoy the journey, and know that when you reach the summit of your Everest, the view will be more amazing, more wonderful and more incredible that you could ever imagine.

APPENDIX

QUIZ ANSWERS

If your score was 20–32:

You would like to be intuitive but you find it hard to distinguish between the insistent voice in your head (your mind) and the more subtle voice of your intuition. You know that at times you are guided by your intuition but are not sure how it happened!

If your score was 33–46:

You know you are intuitive and there are times when you have consciously trusted and acted on your gut feeling, but you have never thought of your intuition as being your personal guidance system. You are open to working with, and being guided by, your intuition on a daily basis and would like to learn more about how to do this, because deep down you know it is your unique voice and that it can help you make the decisions in life that are right for you.

If your score was 47–60:

You are highly intuitive and recognise that your intuition is the voice of who you really are. You know that if you continue to trust and act on its guidance, it will help you to live the life you were born to lead. Although there may still be times when you struggle to trust that subtle voice and to decipher the signals it is giving you, you know that there are no mistakes in life. You also know that being highly tuned in to your inner guide means standing out from the crowd, flowing through life with ease and living the life of your dreams. Who would not want that?!

To find out more about intuition, how to create real change in your life and the future you *really* want visit my Women Have Vision website www.womenhavevision.com

You can also find me on the Women Have Vision Facebook Page and in the Dare To Dream! Facebook group. This is my private group for women who not only dare to dream but are determined to live those dreams. I regularly post videos, coaching tips and intuitive guidance and we all hang out and have fun, because fun is what makes the world go round! So please come and join us there, it's the place to be! https://www.facebook.com/groups/womenhavevisiondaretodream

THE TOOL KIT
FOR UNLOCKING YOUR DREAMS

A combination lock is opened not by a key but by the alignment of all its interior parts.

You are a sum of many parts, which when aligned, create an unstoppable and powerful force that can pull into physical reality whichever of your dreams and desires you wish to apply them to. Used in combination the tools below form the key to unlocking the door to your dreams.

- Your unique gifts
- Intuition
- Feeling good
- Daring to dream
- The secret question
- Imagination

Printed in Great Britain
by Amazon

57293610R00108